SpiritGifts

LEADER'S RESOURCES

SpiritGifts

LEADER'S RESOURCES

PATRICIA D. BROWN

Abingdon Press
Nashville

SPIRITGIFTS: LEADER'S RESOURCES

Copyright © 1996 by Abingdon Press.

This book is printed on acid-free, recycled paper.

Cataloging-in-Publication Data is available from the Library of Congress

ISBN 0-687-00857-3

Scripture quotations are from the New Revised Standard Version Bible, copyright © 1989, by the Division of Christian Education of the National Council of the Churches of Christ in the United States of America. Used by permission.

"Many Gifts, One Spirit," words and music by Al Carmines, is used by permission of the author.

00 01 02 03 04 05 — 10 9 8 7 6

MANUFACTURED IN THE UNITED STATES OF AMERICA

For my gifted son, Stephen Henry Bauman,
the genuine thing, who calls
me to play in life and
lets me be a good
enough mom

Contents

Contents

APPENDIX

Introduction

As a SpiritGifts leader, you have the exciting opportunity of guiding the individuals in your group on a Spirit-led journey of discovery and growth that will empower and equip them for service and leadership in the Body of Christ, the church. In addition to providing a biblical foundation for understanding spiritual gifts and their importance to the church, this program will help the members of your group find God's direction for their lives and increase their sense of meaning and purpose as they name, claim, and come to appreciate their own spiritual gifts. As participants work together to discover their gifts and challenge one another to use those gifts to meet real needs in the local congregation and beyond, your group will experience and build a sense of true community. And as individuals begin to recognize where to focus their energies and become actively involved in serving according to their gifts, the work and ministry of the entire congregation will grow.

Whether your primary purpose is to provide a biblical study of spiritual gifts, empower persons to do God's will in their lives, mobilize individuals for ministries that fit their gifts, spread the work of ministry beyond the "faithful few," nurture persons for leadership, grow a small group or Sunday school class—both numerically and spiritually—or some other goal, you will find SpiritGifts appropriate and adaptable to your unique situation and needs. The materials have been developed in a way that allows you to mold and shape the program according to your preferred leadership style, the resources of space, time, and equipment available to you, and the dynamics of your particular group. Suggestions for leading a SpiritGifts program and specific guides for planning programs of various lengths are provided on pages 10-42.

Whether you follow one of these program guides or create your own, a significant outcome of your group's experience will be the affirmation that each individual is a holy child of God and an important part of God's divine plan. Each individual is gifted by the Spirit. Unlike talents or abilities that can be earned or received through training, spiritual gifts are given to us by God.

Charismata is a Greek word that means gifts of grace. In this program we use the word *charismata* to refer to *all* of the gifts or special abilities given by God. The gifts are given for a purpose; they are intended to be used. The presence of the Holy Spirit energizes our gifts for service. In effect, *charismata* is the call of Jesus Christ to serve within the community, thus benefiting and strengthening the church with the use of specific gifts. *Charismata* is the key that unlocks the power of God to be in ministry to the world.

As you begin this exciting journey, encourage participants to make a commitment to pray for one another. This prayer should center on a constant awareness of the holy within themselves and each person they encounter. Pray that during your time together the Spirit will be at work, helping you to discern God's will in your lives and your ministry.

SpiritGifts sets you and the participants in your group on a course to open yourselves to God in ways that will enable you to see and accept your gifts, which are spiritual realities. The process you begin is open ended. This is only the beginning of an exciting, lifelong journey. May you come to a greater awareness of your own gifts as you help others to know theirs. As you lead, both give and receive, confirm and be confirmed.

How to Lead a SpiritGifts Program

SpiritGifts is intended to be used by persons who want to discover and understand their spiritual gifts and begin to live in ministry with their congregation and community as the Body of Christ. It can be adapted for use by small groups of as few as three or four to large groups of one hundred or more. The following suggestions for implementing and leading a SpiritGifts program are intended to guide your planning for a program tailored to meet the needs of your particular group.

Time, Location, and Atmosphere Are Important.

Find out in advance how much time your participants are willing to give to the program. Then pace the group according to its needs and the desired depth of study. A number of options are available. Session guides for a four-, six,-, nine-, and twelve-week program are provided in this resource. Also included are guidelines for a weekend retreat, one-day workshop, and one-hour session (see pages 15-42). If your group will be meeting over a period of several weeks, set a regular day and time for the weekly session.

Location is also an important consideration. Plan to meet in an area where there will be few interruptions. The room should be large enough for participants to meet as a full group and break into small groups of two to six. (Remember, the more people there are in a small group, the longer it takes to complete an activity.) The best setup includes comfortable chairs and tables strategically placed so that participants may make notes while facing the presentation area.

Atmosphere is also vital to the program. Create a focus center in a central location in the room to remind yourself and the group why you are there: for God's glory. A small table draped with red fabric is appropriate. The color red represents the day of Pentecost, when the Spirit came upon the first Christians. Place a lighted candle on the table as a reminder that the Spirit came as tongues of fire. Choose other symbols that represent the Holy Spirit, such as a dove (a dove lit upon Jesus at his baptism in the Jordan). You also might place a Bible or cross on the table. Be creative, taking care to explain the symbols to the participants. Never assume that they know the origin or meaning of each symbol, or that their understandings are the same as yours.

Another useful tool in creating atmosphere is music. Music can help to set the mood for participants as they arrive. Choose instrumentals or songs that are soothing and reflective. You also may find it helpful to play music softly during some of the reflective exercises and at other times during the session. (See the discussion of **Multimedia** [page 13] for additional suggestions related to music.)

All of the Building Blocks You Need Are Provided.

Although the SpiritGifts resources are arranged according to a certain logic, they are not arranged in a strict sequence. You and your group may choose to use all of the resources provided or identify topics that fit your immediate concerns and interests.

SpiritGifts employs a triple reinforcement technique of "hearing, seeing, and writing." The materials provided in your *Leader's Resources* include the following kinds of pages:

LEADER pages are for your use only. These pages provide important step-by-step instructions, dialogue, and information for use in conducting the program and presenting material to the group. All instructions to you appear within boxes and are marked with a pointing finger. All other text is for you to read aloud to the group. Scripture verses appear in shaded boxes.

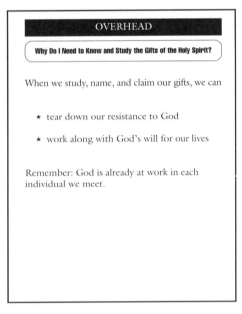

OVERHEAD pages are intended to be used along with the leader pages as visual aids for communicating ideas and information. See the discussion of **Multimedia** (page 13) for more details on how to use these pages.

PARTICIPANT pages are exact reproductions of pages included in the *Participant's Workbook*, provided here for your quick and easy reference when planning and leading a session. Worksheets allow participants to make notes and supply answers. Encourage participants to follow along and fill in their worksheets as you present material. Activity pages challenge participants to reflect on their own spiritual journeys. Use those pages that will help to enhance the spiritual formation of your particular group. Other pages such as a spiritual gifts survey and answer sheet, a personal inventory, and "A Letter to My Congregation" are also provided for your convenient reference.

LEADER/PARTICIPANT pages are included in both the leader and participant books and are provided as important teaching/reference tools to be presented once and then referred to again and again, by the group or by individual participants, as necessary and appropriate throughout the program.

To help make your SpiritGifts program even more effective and enjoyable for you and your participants, a variety of additional tools are provided for your ready use:

Charts—present and summarize information in an easy-to-read format
Prayers—provided in the appendix for use throughout the program
Scriptures—printed in shaded boxes for your convenience
Bible studies—present and explore biblical content using the responsive listening method
Newsletter announcement—can be adapted to publicize your program
Letter to participants—acknowledges participation
Theme song—full music and words to "Many Gifts, One Spirit"
Bibliography of songs—suggested songs to establish mood, reinforce ideas and themes, and involve participants in worship and praise
Bibliography of resources—suggests complementary resources

Multimedia Enhance the Program.

SpiritGifts is much more than a study of spiritual gifts. It is an *experience* of discovery, renewal, and spiritual growth involving study, action, worship, and prayer. The use of a variety of media enhances the effectiveness of the experience.

Music is an integral part of the SpiritGifts experience. As mentioned previously, music can help to create a desired atmosphere and mood. Music also can be used to involve participants in worship and praise, to encourage group participation and fellowship, to reinforce ideas and themes, to signal a change of pace, and to bring the full group back together after a small group activity or break.

The theme song "Many Gifts, One Spirit" is provided on pages 46-47 for your use throughout the program. In addition, an annotated bibliography of suggested songs is provided in the appendix (pages 183-84). If you are fortunate enough to have a musician in your group, the music can be played live. If not, you can record the accompaniment on cassette tape or sing the songs a cappella. If you are not musically inclined, you may want to recruit a song leader as well.

You will find suggestions for when to sing these songs during the program. In addition to these suggestions, feel free to use these and other songs—as well as music on cassettes or CDs—as often as is appropriate and beneficial to your group. When choosing and singing songs, remember that they should inspire and teach. You might want to read some of the songs as poems, or discuss what a song teaches about gifts of the Spirit. You will think of other ways to make music an effective part of your SpiritGifts program.

Overhead transparencies are another useful multimedia tool. Overheads assist you in presenting and communicating ideas effectively. To make overhead transparencies, photocopy the overhead pages from this book onto transparencies, which can be purchased from a local office supply store. Some supply stores can make the transparencies for you. You also will need an overhead projector and a screen that is large enough to accommodate your audience. Space has been provided on the overheads wherever possible for adding information and leader notes. When displaying the overheads, remember to cover the answers, and reveal them one at a time as you proceed, so that your participants do not jump ahead. If overhead equipment is not available, transfer the information from the overhead pages to a flip chart or newsprint.

Video can be an effective supplement to SpiritGifts. An excellent video on spiritual gifts is listed in the *SpiritGifts Bibliography of Resources* (page 185). You may wish to check with your local church organization or agency for additional help in finding videos appropriate for your group.

Name tags will help you conduct sessions in a more personal way for large groups or groups of persons who do not know one another. (Obviously, for smaller groups and long-term groups in which the leader and members know one another well, such as Sunday school classes, name tags are not necessary.) Before the first session, greet and welcome each person as he or she arrives. Print the participant's name on a self-adhesive name tag and place it high on the participant's shoulder. As a courtesy, always ask permission before doing this. Personally distributing the name tags in this way gives you a moment of one-on-one contact with each participant. It also places the tags where you can see them from a distance during the session and recall names as you need them. Depending on the size and makeup of your group, you may want participants to wear name tags at each session or only at the first few sessions.

You Are the Facilitator of the Group.

Your role as group leader is to facilitate the sessions. Being the leader requires no special knowledge, education, or training. You don't have to be a professional Christian educator or pastor to lead Spirit-Gifts. The one attribute you do need is a high commitment to the shared ministry of all believers.

SpiritGifts is designed as a group learning experience. As the group learns together, participants build community. Building trusting and understanding relationships is essential for many of the activities and exercises in the program. Like the leader in *The Story of the Great Teacher* (pages 43-44), you will lead by helping participants "listen and speak and reason together." As this happens, participants become teachers of one another. Through God's Spirit, you become the light of discovery for one another.

Participants are to encourage one another by recognizing, naming, and supporting one another's gifts for ministry. Likewise, it is essential that you remain open and try many ways to use your own gifts to support and strengthen the gifts of others. Not only will you help persons to see themselves as gifted children of God, but you also will encourage participants to see, perhaps for the first time, how spiritual gifts are linked to their daily lives.

As we help persons focus on their gifts for ministry, we also help them discover how those gifts can be used—both inside and outside the church community. Gifts are to be used for God's glory and the furtherance of God's reign in the world wherever we are, with whomever we meet, at whatever place we are in life.

SpiritGifts Is the Beginning of a New Approach to Congregational Ministries.

SpiritGifts can revolutionize your church's approach to meeting the needs of congregational ministries. Unlike administrative structuring that keeps members occupied with filling positions and accomplishing tasks, SpiritGifts can help you to focus members on their appropriate areas of ministry. Now the nominating committee can be replaced with a spiritual gifts committee that invites people to discern and begin to use their gifts through participation in a SpiritGifts group. Participants in these groups not only assist and equip one another but also, using their gifts, reach out in mission as they call one another to service and responsibility.

SpiritGifts also can be used as a powerful way to incorporate new members into the congregation. New members become part of the active community through the study and employment of their gifts. As individuals identify their gifts, they gain a clear understanding of how they can be involved in the life of the church and move out into the wider community.

The gifts of the Spirit enable *all* persons to claim ownership in the work of ministry. As the members of your congregation claim this ownership and begin to use their gifts in community, they will discover that there is a mysterious reciprocity at work in God's plan.

SpiritGifts Program Guides

GETTING READY

Materials:

- *Leader's Resources*
- *Participant's Workbook* for each person
- pencils or pens for each person
- name tags and markers (optional)
- focus center (see page 10)
- live or recorded music and cassette/CD player
- overhead projector and screen, or flip chart and markers, or chalkboard and chalk (as needed)
- VCR and videotapes (optional as supplemental resources)

Setup:

- Arrange the tables or writing surfaces and comfortable chairs.
- Prepare the focus center.
- Set up any audiovisual equipment, such as cassette/CD player, overhead projector and screen, flip chart, or VCR and monitor.
- Have name tags, markers, and participants' workbooks ready.
- Have music playing as participants arrive.

Welcome:

- Call the group together.
- Welcome the participants.
- Introduce yourself (first session only).
- Explain objectives and purpose of the session.

Note: Each of the following program guides references selected materials from the comprehensive SpiritGifts resources. In order to ensure that you meet the needs of your particular group and cover the material important to your purposes, be sure to familiarize yourself with the contents of your *Leader's Resources* so that you may adapt the guides as appropriate for your group.

One-Hour Overview

The one-hour overview is an *introduction* to the SpiritGifts program. The intent is to so excite a group of individuals that they will want to join or begin a SpiritGifts program.

The Big Picture
During the session the group will

- discover that SpiritGifts is a group experience in which all participants become teachers of one another

- consider a definition of "a gift of the Holy Spirit"
- examine three easy steps to finding their gifts
- complete a spiritual gifts survey and list their top three gifts as identified by the survey
- review brief descriptions of the gifts

Action!

		Leader's Resources	Participant's Workbook
1.	Follow the steps outlined in GETTING READY. (Note: The focus center is optional for this session.)	15	
♪ 2.	Sing the theme song, "Many Gifts, One Spirit."	46-47	12-13
3.	Read or retell *The Story of the Great Teacher.*	43-44	
4.	Lead the group in prayer.	182	
◄ 5.	*What Is a Gift of the Holy Spirit?*	70-73	24
◄ 6.	*How Can I Search Out My Gifts?*	74-76	25
7.	*Spiritual Gifts Survey/Answer Sheet.*	88-94	30-35
8.	*My Top Three Gifts.*	95	36
9.	*Gifts of the Spirit: Descriptions.* (Note: See instructions on *Spiritual Gifts Survey: Leader's Resources* page 88.)	96-98	37
10.	Thank the participants and announce when scheduled SpiritGifts programs will be offered, or invite them to begin their own SpiritGifts study.		

One-Day Workshop

A one-day workshop is a good way to introduce and train persons to use SpiritGifts in their own setting or to provide persons the opportunity to participate in a condensed study of the gifts. Your approach will differ according to your participants and expected outcome.

SUGGESTED SCHEDULE

9:00 A.M. – 10:30 A.M.	Session 1	90 minutes
10:30 A.M. – 10:45 A.M.	Break	15 minutes
10:45 A.M. – 12:00 P.M.	Session 2	75 minutes
12:00 P.M. – 1:00 P.M.	Lunch / Discussion Time with Assignment	60 minutes
1:00 P.M. – 2:00 P.M.	Session 3	60 minutes
2:00 P.M. – 2:30 P.M.	Break/Discussion Time with Assignment	30 minutes
2:30 P.M. – 4:00 P.M.	Session 4	90 minutes

SESSION 1

The Big Picture
In this session the group will

- discover that SpiritGifts is a group experience in which all participants become teachers of one another
- learn the significance of the theme song, "Many Gifts, One Spirit," and of the focus center and its symbols
- raise questions they bring to the program
- come to understand that discerning God's will and getting in touch with the work of the Spirit is an ongoing process
- consider a definition of "a gift of the Holy Spirit"
- complete a spiritual gifts survey

Action!

		Leader's Resources	*Participant's Workbook*
	1. Follow the steps outlined in GETTING READY.	15	
	2. Light the candle on the focus center.		
	3. Introduce and sing the theme song, "Many Gifts, One Spirit."	46-47	12-13
	4. Read or retell *The Story of the Great Teacher.*	43-44	
	5. Lead the group in prayer.	182	
	6. *Are These the Questions You Are Asking?*	48-49	14
	7. *Other Questions to Consider.*	50-51	15
	8. *The Work of the Spirit Within You.*	52-56	16-17
	9. *What Is a Gift of the Holy Spirit?*	70-73	24
	10. *Spiritual Gifts Survey/Answer Sheet.*	88-94	30-35
	(Note: Participants may begin their break as they complete the survey.)		

SESSION 2

The Big Picture
In this session the group will

- consider why it is important to know and study the gifts of the Holy Spirit
- learn how they can search out their own gifts
- see how naming and claiming their gifts helps them to live in God's will
- list their top three gifts as identified by the survey and study brief descriptions of eighteen spiritual gifts
- identify their gifts in the context of a community of Christians

Action!

		Leader's Resources	*Participant's Workbook*
	1. Open by singing a verse of "Many Gifts, One Spirit" or another song.	46-47 183-84	12-13
	2. Lead the group in prayer.	182	
	3. *Why Do I Need to Know and Study the Gifts of the Holy Spirit?*	67-69	23
	4. *How Can I Search Out My Gifts?*	74-76	25
	5. *Gifts and God's Will.*	79-83	27-28
	6. *My Top Three Gifts.*	95	36

	Leader's Resources	Participant's Workbook
7. *Gifts of the Spirit: Descriptions.*	96-98	37-41
8. *Discerning Our Gifts in Community.*	125-27	68

(Note: Write the following on newsprint:
"Assignment for lunch discussion:
Find one or more persons who have listed one
of the same top three gifts as you.
Discuss: Why do you think you may have this gift?
What are the evidences of this gift in your life?")

SESSION 3

The Big Picture
In this session the group will

- learn how to distinguish between their own gifts and their roles, works, talents, and abilities
- review key passages in the New Testament related to spiritual gifts
- learn the responsive listening Bible study method
- study 1 Corinthians 12:12-26

Action!

	Leader's Resources	Participant's Workbook
1. Instruct the participants to break into groups of four (make some groups of three if necessary, but do not make any groups of five).		
2. *Gifts Versus Roles and Works of Ministry.*	115-16	63
3. *Gifts Versus Talents and Abilities.*	117-19	64-65
◄ 4. *The Bible and Spiritual Gifts.*	57-59	18
◄ 5. *Some Bible Basics.*	99-103	42-43
6. Introduce *Responsive Listening Bible Study (Eight Steps).*	60-62	19-20
7. *Responsive Listening Bible Study: 1 Corinthians 12:12-26.*	128-31	69-70

SESSION 4

The Big Picture
In this session the group will

- study what it means to be a member of the Body of Christ
- explore together how they may use their gifts in community
- learn how the gifts of the Spirit differ from the "fruits" of the Spirit
- learn four steps to get ready to use their gifts
- claim their gifts by completing a letter to be shared with the congregation
- pray and worship together
- receive certificates of completion

SpiritGifts Program Guides

Action!

		Leader's Resources	Participant's Workbook
	1. Lead the group in prayer.	182	
	2. *The Body of Christ.*	132-35	71
◀	3. *Using Our Gifts in Community.*	142-46	75
	4. *Evidences of Our Gifts Are Found in "Fruits."*	156-57	
◀	5. *Getting Ready to Use Your Gifts.*	158-61	81
	6. *A Letter to My Congregation.*	172-73	86
	7. *Claiming Your Gifts for Ministry.*	170-71	85
	8. *SpiritGifts Covenant and Renewal Service.*	176-80	87-88

   (Note: May be held at a later date in a congregational worship service.)
9. Distribute certificates of completion.

Weekend Retreat

During the weekend retreat, participants will come to understand, name, and claim their gifts for ministry. They will find a clearer sense of God's will and purpose for their lives and be ready to take their rightful place in the life of the church and in mission beyond the local congregation.

Because the program takes place in a retreat setting, a greater emphasis is placed on activities that promote the sharing of personal life experiences and stories.

....

Schedule

Before Retreat Assignment (two weeks in advance)

DAY 1 (FRIDAY)

5:00 P.M. – 6:00 P.M.	Registration and welcome Distribute arrival assignment
6:00 P.M. – 7:00 P.M.	Assignment and dinner
7:00 P.M. – 8:30 P.M.	Session 1
8:30 P.M. – 9:00 P.M.	Bible study 1

DAY 2 (SATURDAY)

8:00 A.M. – 9:00 A.M.	Breakfast
9:00 A.M. – 9:30 A.M.	Bible study 2
9:30 A.M. – 11:00 A.M.	Session 2
11:00 A.M. – 12:00 P.M.	Self-study and reflection
12:00 P.M. – 1:00 P.M.	Lunch

1:00 P.M. –	2:00 P.M.	Self-study and reflection
2:00 P.M. –	3:30 P.M.	Session 3
3:30 P.M. –	4:00 P.M.	Free time
4:00 P.M. –	6:00 P.M.	Bible study 3
6:00 P.M. –	7:00 P.M.	Assignment and dinner
7:00 P.M. –	8:00 P.M.	Session 4
8:00 P.M. –	8:30 P.M.	Bible study 4

DAY 3 (SUNDAY)

8:00 A.M. –	9:00 A.M.	Breakfast
9:00 A.M. –	9:30 A.M.	Self-study and reflection
9:30 A.M. –	10:15 A.M.	Sharing
		Bible study 5
10:15 A.M. –	11:30 A.M.	Session 5
11:30 A.M. –	12:00 P.M.	Self-study and reflection
12:00 P.M. –	1:00 P.M.	Lunch
1:00 P.M. –	2:00 P.M.	Sharing
		Bible study 6
2:00 P.M. –	2:30 P.M.	Self-study and reflection
2:30 P.M. –	3:30 P.M.	Session 6
		SpiritGifts Covenant and Renewal Service

....

Before Retreat Assignment

	Leader's Resources	Participant's Workbook
God Is Always with Me. (Note: Mail or give the participants a letter with instructions for the assignment two weeks before the retreat.)	77-78	26

DAY 1

Registration and Welcome

Assignment on Arrival

	Leader's Resources	Participant's Workbook
As persons register, instruct them to complete the *Spiritual Gifts Survey/Answer Sheet.* (Note: Tell them it should take them approximately twenty minutes to complete.)	88-94	30-35

Dinner
1. Seat the participants at tables of no more than eight persons. Give a general welcome and invite the persons at each table to introduce themselves to one another during the meal. Ask them to share why they have come to the SpiritGifts retreat.
2. Before beginning the meal, lead the group in prayer (see page 182).

SESSION 1

The Big Picture
This session will set the tone for the retreat. Participants will share questions, concerns, and expectations they bring to the retreat. After gaining some basic understandings about SpiritGifts, each participant will share a part of his or her life story with one other person.

Action!

	Leader's Resources	Participant's Workbook
1. Follow the steps outlined in GETTING READY. Invite the participants to introduce themselves to the group.	15	
♪ 2. Introduce and sing the theme song, "Many Gifts, One Spirit."	46-47	12-13
3. Read or retell *The Story of the Great Teacher*.	43-44	
4. Lead the group in prayer.	182	
5. *Are These the Questions You Are Asking?*	48-49	14
◀ 6. *Other Questions to Consider.*	50-51	15
◀ 7. *The Work of the Spirit Within You.*	52-56	16
◀ 8. *What Is a Gift of the Holy Spirit?*	70-73	24
9. *Why Do I Need to Know and Study the Gifts of the Holy Spirit?*	67-69	23
10. *God Is Always with Me.* (Note: participants should have completed their worksheets before the retreat. Invite them to share in pairs.)	77-78	26

Bible Study 1

	Leader's Resources	Participant's Workbook
1. Introduce *Responsive Listening Bible Study (Eight Steps)*.	60-62	19-20
2. *Responsive Listening Bible Study: Ephesians 4:1-16.* (Note: The Bible study groups will remain the same throughout the retreat. A different facilitator will be designated each time the groups meet.)	63-66	21-22
3. Invite the participants to enjoy a relaxing time of snacks and visiting following the Bible study.		

DAY 2

Breakfast

	Leader's Resources	Participant's Workbook
♪ 1. When everyone is seated, sing the theme song, "Many Gifts, One Spirit," or another song.	46-47 183-84	19-20
2. Before beginning the meal, lead the group in prayer.	182	

Bible Study 2

	Leader's Resources	Participant's Workbook
Responsive Listening Bible Study: 1 Corinthians 12:12-26.	128-31	69-70

SESSION 2

The Big Picture
This session builds on the biblical foundation for the program. Participants will gain a clearer understanding of what it means to live in God's will and will begin to explore descriptions and examples of the spiritual gifts.

Action!

		Leader's Resources	Participant's Workbook
	1. Lead the group in prayer.	182	
▶	2. *How Can I Search Out My Gifts?*	74-76	25
▶	3. *The Bible and Spiritual Gifts.*	57-59	18
▶	4. *Some Bible Basics.*	99-103	42-43
▶	5. *Gifts and God's Will.*	79-83	27-28
	6. *Spiritual Gifts Survey/Answer Sheet.*	88-94	30-35
	7. *My Top Three Gifts.*	95	36
	8. *Gifts of the Spirit: Descriptions.*	96-98	37-41
	9. Give the assignment for self-study and reflection time: *Biblical and Contemporary Examples of the Gifts* (see below).	104-14	44-62

Self-Study and Reflection
Participants should read *Biblical and Contemporary Examples of the Gifts* and reflect on other examples of the gifts in their own and others' lives.

Lunch

	Leader's Resources	Participant's Workbook
1. When everyone is seated, sing a song of your choice.	183-84	
2. Give instructions for the self-study and reflection time to follow lunch: *Patterns of My Life* (see below).	123-24	67
3. Before beginning the meal, lead the group in prayer.	182	

Self-Study and Reflection
During lunch, each participant should choose a partner for the activity *Patterns of My Life*. Each pair should agree on a time to come together and complete part B of the exercise.

SESSION 3

The Big Picture
In this session participants will differentiate between their gifts and the roles, works, talents, and abilities they have. They will examine life activities that bring them joy in order to find clues about their gifts, and they will discover how their lives are different when they live in God's will.

Action!

	Leader's Resources	Participant's Workbook
1. Lead the group in prayer.	182	

	Leader's Resources	Participant's Workbook
2. *Gifts Versus Roles and Works of Ministry.*	115-16	63
3. *Gifts Versus Talents and Abilities.*	117-19	64-65
▶ 4. *What Will the Gift Look Like When I See It?*	120-22	66
5. *Patterns of My Life.* (Note: Participants completed this activity during the self-study and reflection time and should be ready to share their reflections.)	123-24	67
▶ 6. *When I Live in God's Will.* (Note: Begin free time after this exercise.)	84-87	29

Bible Study 3

	Leader's Resources	Participant's Workbook
1. *Responsive Listening Bible Study: Romans 12:3-8.*	147-48	76
2. Dismiss from small groups.		

Dinner

	Leader's Resources	Participant's Workbook
1. Ask participants to remain standing as everyone enters the dining room and to wait for further instructions.		
2. Instruct each participant to find one other person who has listed one of the same top three gifts as he or she, and to discuss the questions found on *Discerning Our Gifts in Community* during dinner.	125-27	68
3. When everyone is seated, lead the group in prayer.	182	

SESSION 4

The Big Picture
This session explores how persons use their gifts in community to be a part of the Body of Christ.

Action!

	Leader's Resources	Participant's Workbook
♪ 1. Sing a song of your choice.	183-84	
2. Lead the group in prayer.	182	
▶ 3. *The Body of Christ.*	132-35	71
4. *I Am a Part of the Body of Christ.*	136-37	72
▶ 5. *Using Our Gifts in Community.*	142-46	75
6. Invite participants to join in a relaxing time of snacks and visiting following the Bible study.		

Bible Study 4

	Leader's Resources	Participant's Workbook
1. *Responsive Listening Bible Study: 1 Corinthians 13.*	138-39	73
2. Participants will break from their small groups.		

DAY 3

Breakfast

	Leader's Resources	Participant's Workbook
♪ 1. When everyone is seated, sing a song of your choice.	183-84	
2. Announce the assignment for the self-study and reflection time following breakfast: *Strive for the Greater Gifts* (see below).	140-41	74
3. Lead the group in prayer.	182	

Self-Study and Reflection

Participants should spend the full thirty minutes reflecting on the lives of five people they know or have known whose lives are centered in love. Instruct them to make notes on their worksheets for sharing with the full group.

Sharing/Bible Study 5

	Leader's Resources	Participant's Workbook
1. *Strive for the Greater Gifts.* (Note: Participants should be prepared to share their reflections and writings.)	140-41	74
2. *Responsive Listening Bible Study: Matthew 7:15-20; Galatians 5:22-25.*	154-55	80

SESSION 5

The Big Picture

In this session participants will prayerfully name the gifts they perceive in one another and tell why. They will learn how the gifts of the Spirit differ from the "fruits" of the Spirit. Finally, each participant will take a quick inventory of the gifts he or she has discerned and will prepare to use them.

Action!

	Leader's Resources	Participant's Workbook
1. Lead the group in prayer.	182	
2. *Naming One Another's Gifts.*	149-51	77-78
3. *Evidences of Our Gifts Are Found in "Fruits."*	156-57	
◄ 4. *Getting Ready to Use Your Gifts.*	158-61	81
5. *A Quick Inventory.*	162-63	82
6. Announce the assignment for self-study and reflection: *A Blessed Healing* (see below).	164-65	83

Self-Study and Reflection

Have participants complete their worksheets individually, without any prior introductory comments. Share the material on the leader page with the full group after lunch.

Lunch

	Leader's Resources	Participant's Workbook
♪ 1. When participants are seated, sing a song of your choice.	183-84	
2. Lead the group in prayer.	182	

Sharing/Bible Study 6

	Leader's Resources	Participant's Workbook
1. *A Blessed Healing.* (Note: Share the information provided on the leader page before having participants share their responses to the activity.)	164-65	83
2. *Responsive Listening Bible Study: Romans 12:3-8.*	147-48	76
3. Announce the assignments for self-study and reflection: *Claiming Your Gifts for Ministry* and *A Letter to My Congregation* (see below).	170-71, 172-73	85, 86

Self-Study and Reflection

Instruct participants to complete *Claiming Your Gifts for Ministry* first and then move on to *A Letter to My Congregation.* Tell them in advance how the letters will be used.

SESSION 6/SpiritGifts Covenant and Renewal Service

The Big Picture
In this session participants will share their letters naming and claiming their gifts for ministry. The retreat will end with the *SpiritGifts Covenant and Renewal Service.*

Action!

	Leader's Resources	Participant's Workbook
1. Lead the group in prayer.	182	
2. *A Letter to My Congregation.* (Note: Have participants share as they will or display the letters on a board or wall.)	172-73	86
3. *Claiming Your Gifts for Ministry.* (Note: Break into small groups and continue the exercise.)	170-71	85
4. *Guided Prayer: Breathing in the Holy Spirit.*	168-69	
5. *SpiritGifts Covenant and Renewal Service.*	176-80	87-88
6. Distribute certificates of completion.	175	

Four-Week Program
(Allow 1–1½ hours for each session.)

SESSION 1

The Big Picture
In this session the group will

- discover that SpiritGifts is a group experience in which all participants become teachers of one another

- learn the significance of the theme song, "Many Gifts, One Spirit," and of the focus center and its symbols
- come to understand that discerning God's will and getting in touch with the work of the Spirit is an ongoing process
- recognize that the focus of SpiritGifts is on how the Holy Spirit empowers and equips us for the work of ministry within the Christian community
- review key passages in the New Testament related to spiritual gifts
- study Ephesians 4:1-16

Action!

		Leader's Resources	Participant's Workbook
	1. Follow the steps outlined in GETTING READY.	15	
🕯	2. Light the candle on the focus center and explain the significance of the symbols displayed there.		
♪	3. Introduce and sing the theme song, "Many Gifts, One Spirit."	46-47	12-13
	4. Read or retell *The Story of the Great Teacher.*	43-44	
	5. Lead the group in prayer.	182	
🔊	6. *The Work of the Spirit Within You.*	52-56	16-17
🔊	7. *The Bible and Spiritual Gifts.*	57-59	18
	8. Introduce *Responsive Listening Bible Study (Eight Steps).*	60-62	19-20
	9. *Responsive Listening Bible Study: Ephesians 4:1-16.*	63-66	21-22
	10. Dismiss from small groups.		

SESSION 2

The Big Picture
In this session the group will

- consider a definition of "a gift of the Holy Spirit"
- explore how spiritual gifts are a part of God's will for their lives and what happens when they live in God's will
- complete a spiritual gifts survey and list their three primary gifts as identified by the survey
- review brief descriptions of eighteen spiritual gifts

Action!

		Leader's Resources	Participant's Workbook
	1. Follow the steps outlined in GETTING READY.	15	
🕯	2. Light the candle on the focus center.		
♪	3. Sing the theme song, "Many Gifts, One Spirit," and/or another song.	46-47, 183-84	12-13
	4. Lead the group in prayer.	182	
🔊	5. *What Is a Gift of the Holy Spirit?*	70-73	24
🔊	6. *Gifts and God's Will.*	79-83	27-28
🔊	7. *When I Live in God's Will.*	84-87	29
	8. *Spiritual Gifts Survey/Answer Sheet.*	88-94	30-35
	9. *My Top Three Gifts.*	95	36

	Leader's Resources	Participant's Workbook
10. *Gifts of the Spirit: Descriptions.*	96-98	37-41
11. Close with prayer.	182	

SESSION 3

The Big Picture

In this session the group will

- discover some Bible basics related to the gifts of the Spirit
- learn how to distinguish between their own gifts and their roles, works, talents, and abilities
- work in pairs to identify evidences of their gifts
- examine their gifts with others who share those gifts

Action!

		Leader's Resources	Participant's Workbook
	1. Follow the steps outlined in GETTING READY.	15	
🕯	2. Light the candle on the focus center.		
♪	3. Sing the theme song, "Many Gifts, One Spirit," and/or another song.	46-47, 183-84	12-13
	4. Lead the group in prayer.	182	
🎞	5. *Some Bible Basics.*	99-103	42-43
	6. *Gifts Versus Roles and Works of Ministry.*	115-16	63
	7. *Gifts Versus Talents and Abilities.*	117-19	64-65
🎞	8. *What Will the Gift Look Like When I See It?*	120-22	66
	9. *Discerning Our Gifts in Community.*	125-27	68
	10. Close with prayer.	182	

SESSION 4

The Big Picture

In this session the group will

- study what it means to be a member of the Body of Christ
- explore together how they may use their gifts in community
- study 1 Corinthians 12:12-26
- claim their gifts by completing letters to be shared with the congregation

Action!

		Leader's Resources	Participant's Workbook
	1. Follow the steps outlined in GETTING READY.	15	
🕯	2. Light the candle on the focus center.		
♪	3. Sing the theme song, "Many Gifts, One Spirit," and/or another song.	46-47, 183-84	12-13

		Leader's Resources	Participant's Workbook
◄	4. Lead the group in prayer.	182	
◄	5. *The Body of Christ.*	132-35	71
◄	6. *Using Our Gifts in Community.*	142-46	75
	7. *Responsive Listening Bible Study: 1 Corinthians 12:12-26.*	128-31	76
	8. *A Letter to My Congregation.*	172-73	86
	9. Close with prayer.	182	

Six-Week Program

(Allow 1–1½ hours for each session.)

SESSION 1

The Big Picture
In this session the group will

- discover that SpiritGifts is a group experience in which all participants become teachers of one another
- learn the significance of the theme song, "Many Gifts, One Spirit," and of the focus center and its symbols
- raise questions they bring to the program
- come to understand that discerning God's will and getting in touch with the work of the Spirit is an ongoing process
- recognize that the focus of SpiritGifts is on how the Holy Spirit empowers and equips us for the work of ministry within the Christian community
- study Ephesians 4:1-16

Action!

		Leader's Resources	Participant's Workbook
	1. Follow the steps outlined in GETTING READY.	15	
🕯	2. Light the candle on the focus center and explain the significance of the symbols displayed there.		
♪	3. Introduce and sing the theme song, "Many Gifts, One Spirit."	46-47	12-13
	4. Read or retell *The Story of the Great Teacher.*	43-44	
	5. Lead the group in prayer.	182	
	6. *Are These the Questions You Are Asking?*	48-49	14
	7. *Other Questions to Consider.*	50-51	15
◄	8. *The Work of the Spirit Within You.*	52-56	16-17
	9. Introduce *Responsive Listening Bible Study (Eight Steps).*	60-62	19-20
	10. *Responsive Listening Bible Study: Ephesians 4:1-16.*	63-66	21-22
	11. Dismiss from small groups.		

SESSION 2

The Big Picture
In this session the group will

- consider a definition of "a gift of the Holy Spirit"
- complete a spiritual gifts survey and list their three primary gifts as identified by the survey
- study brief descriptions of eighteen spiritual gifts

Action!

		Leader's Resources	Participant's Workbook
1.	Follow the steps outlined in GETTING READY.	15	
2.	Light the candle on the focus center.		
3.	Sing the theme song, "Many Gifts, One Spirit," and/or another song.	46-47, 183-84	12-13
4.	Lead the group in prayer.	182	
5.	*What Is a Gift of the Holy Spirit?*	70-73	24
6.	*Spiritual Gifts Survey/Answer Sheet.*	88-94	30-35
7.	*My Top Three Gifts.*	95	36
8.	*Gifts of the Spirit: Descriptions.*	96-98	37-41
9.	Close with prayer.	182	

SESSION 3

The Big Picture
In this session the group will

- see how naming and claiming their gifts helps them to live in God's will
- consider what happens when they live in God's will for their lives
- examine three easy steps to finding their gifts
- recognize times and ways that God breaks into their daily lives

Action!

		Leader's Resources	Participant's Workbook
1.	Follow the steps outlined in GETTING READY.	15	
2.	Light the candle on the focus center.		
3.	Sing the theme song, "Many Gifts, One Spirit," and/or another song.	46-47, 183-84	12-13
4.	Lead the group in prayer.	182	
5.	*Gifts and God's Will.*	79-83	
6.	*When I Live in God's Will.*	84-87	27-28
7.	*How Can I Search Out My Gifts?*	74-76	29
8.	*God Is Always with Me.*	77-78	26
9.	Close with prayer.	182	

SESSION 4

The Big Picture
In this session the group will

- discover some Bible basics related to the gifts of the Spirit
- learn how to distinguish between their own gifts and their roles, works, talents, and abilities
- work in pairs to identify evidences of their gifts
- examine their gifts with others who share those gifts

Action!

		Leader's Resources	Participant's Workbook
	1. Follow the steps outlined in GETTING READY.	15	
	2. Light the candle on the focus center.		
	3. Sing the theme song, "Many Gifts, One Spirit," and/or another song.	46-47, 183-84	12-13
	4. Lead the group in prayer.	182	
	5. *Some Bible Basics.*	99-103	42-43
	6. *Gifts Versus Roles and Works of Ministry.*	115-16	63
	7. *Gifts Versus Talents and Abilities.*	117-19	64-65
	8. *What Will the Gift Look Like When I See It?*	120-22	66
	9. *Discerning Our Gifts in Community.*	125-27	68
	10. Close with prayer.	182	

SESSION 5

The Big Picture
In this session the group will

- name the gifts they see in others
- recognize the "fruits" of spiritual gifts
- study Matthew 7:12-20 and Galatians 5:22-25

Action!

		Leader's Resources	Participant's Workbook
	1. Follow the steps outlined in GETTING READY.	15	
	2. Light the candle on the focus center.		
	3. Sing the theme song, "Many Gifts, One Spirit," and/or another song.	46-47, 183-84	12-13
	4. Lead the group in prayer.	182	
	5. *Naming One Another's Gifts.*	149-51	77
	6. *Responsive Listening Bible Study: Matthew 7:15-20; Galatians 5:22-25.*	154-55	80
	7. *Evidences of Our Gifts Are Found in "Fruits."*	156-57	
	8. Close with prayer.	182	

SESSION 6

The Big Picture
In this session the group will

- study what it means to be a member of the Body of Christ
- explore together how they may use their gifts in community
- study 1 Corinthians 12:12-26
- claim their gifts by completing letters to be shared with the congregation

Action!

		Leader's Resources	*Participant's Workbook*
	1. Follow the steps outlined in GETTING READY.	15	
	2. Light the candle on the focus center.		
	3. Sing the theme song, "Many Gifts, One Spirit," and/or another song.	46-47, 183-84	12-13
	4. Lead the group in prayer.	182	
	5. *The Body of Christ.*	132-35	71
	6. *Using Our Gifts in Community.*	142-46	75
	7. *Responsive Listening Bible Study: 1 Corinthians 12:12-26.*	128-31	69-70
	8. *A Letter to My Congregation.*	172-173	86
	9. Close with prayer.	182	

Nine-Week Program
(Allow 1–1½ hours for each session.)

SESSION 1

The Big Picture
In this session the group will
- discover that SpiritGifts is a group experience in which all participants become teachers of one another
- learn the significance of the theme song, "Many Gifts, One Spirit," and of the focus center and its symbols
- raise questions they bring to the program
- review key passages in the New Testament related to spiritual gifts
- study Ephesians 4:1-16

Action!

		Leader's Resources	*Participant's Workbook*
	1. Follow the steps outlined in GETTING READY.	15	
	2. Light the candle on the focus center and explain the significance of the symbols displayed there.		
	3. Introduce and sing the theme song, "Many Gifts, One Spirit."	46-47	12-13

		Leader's Resources	Participant's Workbook
4.	Read or retell *The Story of the Great Teacher*.	43-44	
5.	Lead the group in prayer.	182	
6.	*Are These the Questions You Are Asking?*	48-49	14
7.	*Other Questions to Consider.*	50-51	15
8.	*The Bible and Spiritual Gifts.*	57-59	18
9.	Introduce *Responsive Listening Bible Study (Eight Steps)*.	60-62	19-20
10.	*Responsive Listening Bible Study: Ephesians 4:1-16.*	63-66	21-22
11.	Dismiss from small groups.		

SESSION 2

The Big Picture
In this session the group will

- consider why it is important to know and study the gifts of the Holy Spirit
- come to understand that discerning God's will and getting in touch with the work of the Spirit is an ongoing process
- recognize that the focus of *SpiritGifts* is on how the Holy Spirit empowers and equips us for the work of ministry within the Christian community
- consider a definition of "a gift of the Holy Spirit"
- learn how they can search out their own gifts
- reflect on times and places they have recognized God's presence in their lives

Action!

		Leader's Resources	Participant's Workbook
1.	Follow the steps outlined in GETTING READY.	15	
2.	Light the candle on the focus center.		
3.	Sing the theme song, "Many Gifts, One Spirit," and/or another song.	46-47, 183-84	12-13
4.	Lead the group in prayer.	182	
5.	*The Work of the Spirit Within You.*	52-56	16
6.	*Why Do I Need to Know and Study the Gifts of the Holy Spirit?*	67-69	23
7.	*What Is a Gift of the Holy Spirit?*	70-73	24
8.	*How Can I Search Out My Gifts?*	74-76	25
9.	*God Is Always with Me.*	77-78	26
10.	Close with prayer.	182	

SESSION 3

The Big Picture
In this session the group will

- see how naming and claiming their gifts helps them to live in God's will
- consider what happens when they live in God's will for their lives

- complete a spiritual gifts survey and list their three primary gifts as identified by the survey
- study brief descriptions of eighteen spiritual gifts

Action!

		Leader's Resources	Participant's Workbook
	1. Follow the steps outlined in GETTING READY.	15	
	2. Light the candle on the focus center.		
	3. Sing the theme song, "Many Gifts, One Spirit," and/or another song.	46-47, 183-84	12-13
	4. Lead the group in prayer.	182	
	5. *Gifts and God's Will.*	79-83	27-28
	6. *When I Live in God's Will.*	84-87	29
	7. *Spiritual Gifts Survey/Answer Sheet.*	88-94	30-35
	8. *My Top Three Gifts.*	95	36
	9. *Gifts of the Spirit: Descriptions.*	96-98	37-41
	10. Close with prayer.	182	

SESSION 4

The Big Picture
In this session the group will

- discover some Bible basics related to the gifts of the Spirit
- learn how to distinguish between their own gifts and their roles, works, talents, and abilities
- work in pairs to identify evidences of their gifts

Action!

		Leader's Resources	Participant's Workbook
	1. Follow the steps outlined in GETTING READY.	15	
	2. Light the candle on the focus center.		
	3. Sing the theme song, "Many Gifts, One Spirit," and/or another song.	46-47, 183-84	12-13
	4. Lead the group in prayer.	182	
	5. *Some Bible Basics.*	99-103	42-43
	6. *Gifts Versus Roles and Works of Ministry.*	115-16	63
	7. *Gifts Versus Talents and Abilities.*	117-19	64-65
	8. *What Will the Gift Look Like When I See It?*	120-22	66
	9. Close with prayer.	182	

SESSION 5

The Big Picture
In this session the group will

- gain a better understanding of the Body of Christ

- identify their gifts in the context of a community of Christians
- study 1 Corinthians 12:12-26

Action!

		Leader's Resources	Participant's Workbook
	1. Follow the steps outlined in GETTING READY.	15	
	2. Light the candle on the focus center.		
	3. Sing the theme song, "Many Gifts, One Spirit," and/or another song.	46-47, 183-84	12-13
	4. *Discerning Our Gifts in Community.*	125-27	68
	5. *I Am a Part of the Body of Christ.*	136-37	72
	6. *Responsive Listening Bible Study: 1 Corinthians 12:12-26.*	128-31	69-70
	7. Dismiss from small groups.		

SESSION 6

The Big Picture
In this session the group will

- discover what it means to be a member of the Body of Christ
- explore together how they may use their gifts in community
- study Romans 12:3-8

Action!

		Leader's Resources	Participant's Workbook
	1. Follow the steps outlined in GETTING READY.	15	
	2. Light the candle on the focus center.		
	3. Sing the theme song, "Many Gifts, One Spirit," and/or another song.	46-47, 183-84	12-13
	4. Lead the group in prayer.	182	
	5. *The Body of Christ.*	132-35	71
	6. *Using Our Gifts in Community.*	142-46	75
	7. *Responsive Listening Bible Study: Romans 12:3-8.*	147-48	76
	8. Dismiss from small groups.		

SESSION 7

The Big Picture
In this session the group will

- name the gifts they perceive in one another and tell why
- share in pairs what gives their lives passion and meaning in order to find clues about their gifts

Action!

		Leader's Resources	Participant's Workbook
	1. Follow the steps outlined in GETTING READY.	15	

		Leader's Resources	Participant's Workbook
🕯	2. Light the candle on the focus center.		
♪	3. Sing the theme song, "Many Gifts, One Spirit," and/or another song.	46-47, 183-84	12-13
	4. Lead the group in prayer.	182	
	5. *Naming One Another's Gifts.*	149-51	77-78
	6. *A Passion for God's Purpose.*	152-53	79
	7. Close with prayer.	182	

SESSION 8

The Big Picture
In this session the group will

- learn four steps to get ready to use their gifts
- study the fruits of the Spirit
- prayerfully claim their gifts in community

Action!

		Leader's Resources	Participant's Workbook
	1. Follow the steps outlined in GETTING READY.	15	
🕯	2. Light the candle on the focus center.		
♪	3. Sing the theme song, "Many Gifts, One Spirit," and/or another song.	46-47, 183-84	12-13
	4. Lead the group in prayer.	182	
📢	5. *Getting Ready to Use Your Gifts.*	158-61	81
	6. *Evidences of Our Gifts Are Found in "Fruits."*	156-57	
	7. *Claiming Your Gifts for Ministry.*	170-71	85
	8. Dismiss from small groups.		

SESSION 9

The Big Picture
In this session the group will

- study Acts 1:1-8
- claim their gifts by completing letters to be shared with the congregation
- participate in a guided prayer
- share a special blessing with one another
- receive certificates of completion

Action!

		Leader's Resources	Participant's Workbook
	1. Follow the steps outlined in GETTING READY.	15	

		Leader's Resources	Participant's Workbook
🕯	2. Light the candle on the focus center.		
♪	3. Sing the theme song, "Many Gifts, One Spirit," and/or another song.	46-47, 183-84	12-13
	4. Lead the group in prayer.	182	
	5. *Responsive Listening Bible Study: Acts 1:1-8.*	166-67	84
	6. *A Letter to My Congregation.*	172-73	86
	7. *Guided Prayer: Breathing in the Holy Spirit.*	168-69	
	8. *SpiritGifts Covenant and Renewal Service: The Blessing.*	177-78	87-88
	9. Give a certificate of completion to each participant.	175	

Twelve-Week Program
(Allow 1–1½ hours for each session.)

SESSION 1

The Big Picture
In this session the group will

- discover that SpiritGifts is a group experience in which all participants become teachers of one another
- learn the significance of the theme song, "Many Gifts, One Spirit," and of the focus center and its symbols
- raise questions they bring to the program
- come to understand that discerning God's will and getting in touch with the work of the Spirit is an ongoing process
- recognize that the focus of SpiritGifts is on how the Holy Spirit empowers and equips us for the work of ministry within the Christian community

Action!

		Leader's Resources	Participant's Workbook
	1. Follow the steps outlined in GETTING READY.	15	
🕯	2. Light the candle on the focus center.		
♪	3. Introduce and sing the theme song, "Many Gifts, One Spirit."	46-47	12-13
	4. Read or retell *The Story of the Great Teacher.*	43-44	
	5. Lead the group in prayer.	182	
	6. *Are These the Questions You Are Asking?*	48-49	14
	7. *Other Questions to Consider.*	50-51	15
📖	8. *The Work of the Spirit Within You.*	52-56	16-17
	9. Close with prayer.	182	

SESSION 2

The Big Picture
In this session the group will

- consider why it is important to know and study the gifts of the Holy Spirit
- consider a definition of "a gift of the Holy Spirit"
- examine three easy steps to finding their gifts
- review key passages in the New Testament related to spiritual gifts

Action!

		Leader's Resources	Participant's Workbook
	1. Follow the steps outlined in GETTING READY.	15	
	2. Light the candle on the focus center.		
	3. Sing the theme song, "Many Gifts, One Spirit," and/or another song.	46-47, 183-84	12-13
	4. Lead the group in prayer.	182	
	5. *Why Do I Need to Know and Study the Gifts of the Holy Spirit?*	67-69	23
	6. *What Is a Gift of the Holy Spirit?*	70-73	24
	7. *How Can I Search Out My Gifts?*	74-76	25
	8. *The Bible and Spiritual Gifts.*	57-59	18
	9. Close with prayer.	182	

SESSION 3

The Big Picture
In this session the group will

- discover some Bible basics related to the gifts of the Spirit
- study Ephesians 4:1-16

Action!

		Leader's Resources	Participant's Workbook
	1. Follow the steps outlined in GETTING READY.	15	
	2. Light the candle on the focus center.		
	3. Sing the theme song, "Many Gifts, One Spirit," and/or another song.	46-47, 183-84	12-13
	4. Lead the group in prayer.	182	
	5. *Some Bible Basics.*	99-103	42-43
	6. Introduce *Responsive Listening Bible Study (Eight Steps).*	60-62	19-20
	7. *Responsive Listening Bible Study: Ephesians 4:1-16.*	63-66	21-22
	8. Close with a song and the Lord's Prayer or another closing prayer.	182-84	

SESSION 4

The Big Picture
In this session the group will

- see how naming and claiming their gifts helps them to live in God's will
- recognize times and ways that God breaks into their daily lives

• complete a spiritual gifts survey and list their three primary gifts as identified by the survey

Action!

		Leader's Resources	Participant's Workbook
	1. Follow the steps outlined in GETTING READY.	15	
	2. Light the candle on the focus center.		
	3. Sing the theme song, "Many Gifts, One Spirit," and/or another song.	46-47, 183-84	12-13
	4. Lead the group in prayer.	182	
	5. *Gifts and God's Will.*	79-83	27-28
	6. *God Is Always with Me.*	77-78	26
	7. *Spiritual Gifts Survey/Answer Sheet.*	88-94	30-35
	8. *My Top Three Gifts.*	95	36
	9. Close with prayer.	182	

SESSION 5

The Big Picture
In this session the group will

• study brief descriptions of eighteen spiritual gifts
• consider biblical and contemporary examples of persons who show evidences of the gifts

Action!

		Leader's Resources	Participant's Workbook
	1. Follow the steps outlined in GETTING READY.	15	
	2. Light the candle on the focus center.		
	3. Sing the theme song, "Many Gifts, One Spirit," and/or another song.	46-47, 183-84	12-13
	4. Lead the group in prayer.	182	
	5. *Gifts of the Spirit: Descriptions.*	96-98	37-41
	6. *Biblical and Contemporary Examples of the Gifts.*	104-14	44-62
	7. Close with prayer.	182	

SESSION 6

The Big Picture
In this session the group will

- work in pairs to identify activities and events that reveal patterns of God's activity in their lives
- consider what happens when they live in God's will for their lives
- learn how to distinguish between their own gifts and their roles, works, talents, and abilities
- work in pairs to identify evidences of their gifts

Action!

		Leader's Resources	Participant's Workbook
	1. Follow the steps outlined in GETTING READY.	15	
	2. Light the candle on the focus center.		
♪	3. Sing the theme song, "Many Gifts, One Spirit," and/or another song.	46-47, 183-84	12-13
	4. Lead the group in prayer.	182	
	5. *Gifts Versus Roles and Works of Ministry.*	115-16	63
	6. *Gifts Versus Talents and Abilities.*	117-19	64-65
	7. *What Will the Gift Look Like When I See It?*	120	66
	8. *When I Live in God's Will.*	84-87	29
	9. Dismiss from small groups.		

SESSION 7

The Big Picture
In this session the group will

- examine their gifts with others who share those gifts.
- gain a better understanding of the Body of Christ
- discover what it means to be a member of the Body of Christ
- study 1 Corinthians 12:12-26

Action!

		Leader's Resources	Participant's Workbook
	1. Follow the steps outlined in GETTING READY.	15	
	2. Light the candle on the focus center.		
♪	3. Sing the theme song, "Many Gifts, One Spirit," and/or another song.	46-47, 183-84	12-13
	4. Lead the group in prayer.	182	
	5. Discerning Our Gifts in Community	125-27	68
	6. *The Body of Christ.*	132-35	71
	7. *I Am a Part of the Body of Christ.*	136-37	72
	8. *Responsive Listening Bible Study: 1 Corinthians 12:12-26.*	128-31	69-70
	9. Dismiss from small groups.		

SESSION 8

The Big Picture
In this session the group will

- discover how SpiritGifts can be foundational to the ongoing work of congregational ministry
- invite one another to name, claim, and use their gifts
- explore how, through the work of the Spirit, individuals mature in faith and power struggles between individuals and groups end

Action!

		Leader's Resources	Participant's Workbook
	1. Follow the steps outlined in GETTING READY.	15	
	2. Light the candle on the focus center.		
	3. Sing the theme song, "Many Gifts, One Spirit," and/or another song.	46-47, 183-84	12-13
	4. Lead the group in prayer.	182	
	5. *Using Our Gifts in Community.*	142-46	75
	6. *Strive for the Greater Gifts.*	140-41	74
	7. *Responsive Listening Bible Study: 1 Corinthians 13.*	138-39	73

SESSION 9

The Big Picture
In this session the group will

- study Romans 12:3-8
- name the gifts they perceive in one another and tell why
- share in pairs what gives their lives passion and meaning in order to find clues about their gifts

Action!

		Leader's Resources	Participant's Workbook
	1. Follow the steps outlined in GETTING READY.	15	
	2. Light the candle on the focus center.		
	3. Sing the theme song, "Many Gifts, One Spirit," and/or another song.	46-47, 183-84	12-13
	4. Lead the group in prayer.	182	
	5. *Responsive Listening Bible Study: Romans 12:3-8.*	147-48	76
	6. *Naming One Another's Gifts.*	149-51	77-78
	7. *A Passion for God's Purpose.*	152-53	79
	8. Close with prayer.	182	

SESSION 10

The Big Picture
In this session the group will

- learn how the gifts of the Spirit differ from the "fruits" of the Spirit
- study Matthew 7:15-20 and Galatians 5:22-25
- learn four steps to get ready to use their gifts

	Leader's Resources	Participant's Workbook
1. Follow the steps outlined in GETTING READY.	15	
2. Light the candle on the focus center.		
3. Sing the theme song, "Many Gifts, One Spirit," and/or another song.	46-47 183-84	12-13
4. Lead the group in prayer.	182	
5. *Evidences of Our Gifts Are Found in "Fruits."*	156-57	
6. *Responsive Listening Bible Study: Matthew 7:15-20; Galatians 5:22-25.*	154-55	80
7. *Getting Ready to Use Your Gifts.*	158-61	81
8. Close with prayer.	182	

SESSION 11

The Big Picture
In this session the group will

- review the gifts they have named and claimed and consider present and future uses of those gifts
- gain new understanding of how they might use their gifts in ministry with others as they reflect on experiences of healing
- study Acts 1:1-8

Action!

	Leader's Resources	Participant's Workbook
1. Follow the steps outlined in GETTING READY.	15	
2. Light the candle on the focus center.		
3. Sing the theme song, "Many Gifts, One Spirit," and/or another song.	46-47, 183-84	12-13
4. Lead the group in prayer.	182	
5. *A Quick Inventory.*	162-63	82
6. *A Blessed Healing.*	164-65	83
7. *Responsive Listening Bible Study: Acts 1:1-8.*	166-67	84
8. Close with prayer.	182	

SESSION 12

The Big Picture
In this session the group will

- participate in a guided prayer
- prayerfully claim their gifts in community
- formally claim their gifts by completing letters to be shared with the congregation
- receive certificates of completion

SpiritGifts: Leader's Resources

		Leader's Resources	Participant's Workbook
1.	Follow the steps outlined in GETTING READY.	15	
2.	Light the candle on the focus center.		
3.	Sing the theme song, "Many Gifts, One Spirit," and/or another song.	46-47, 183-84	12-13
4.	Lead the group in prayer.	182	
5.	*Guided Prayer: Breathing in the Holy Spirit.*	168-69	
6.	*Claiming Your Gifts for Ministry.*	170-71	85
7.	*A Letter to My Congregation.*	172-73	86
8.	Close with the *SpiritGifts Covenant and Renewal Service*, or if the service is scheduled for a congregational worship service, close with the theme song and prayer.	176-80, 46-47, 182	87-88 12-13

The Story of the Great Teacher*

☞ Telling *The Story of the Great Teacher* sets the stage for the SpiritGifts program. In order to prepare yourself to tell the story, read the text several times until you are familiar with it. Then practice retelling the story several times. Be as dramatic and creative as you like so that the story will become a memorable part of the participants' experience.

There once was a Great Teacher. A community heard of the Great Teacher, and the wisdom and knowledge she possessed, and decided to ask the Great Teacher to come and speak to them. The Great Teacher agreed to come. On the designated day, she came, stood before them, opened her book, and said, "Do you know what I've come to say to you today?" The group, thinking this a simplistic question, shook their heads, saying, "No."

"Well, then I will not waste my time on so ignorant a group," the Great Teacher said as she closed her book and left.

The community, shaken but not disheartened, invited the Great Teacher to come a second time. On the designated day the Great Teacher came, stood before them, opened her book, and said, "Do you know what I've come to say to you today?" The group, remembering their previous experience, said, "Yes."

"Well, if you already know, you don't need me." And she closed her book and left.

The community believed that the Great Teacher had something important to say to them. With even more determination, they decided to ask the Great Teacher to come once again. Now, they must have been (denomination or church name), because they formed a committee to discuss the problem. After much deliberation, they came up with a plan; and they invited the Great Teacher once again. On the designated day the Great Teacher came, stood before them, opened her book, and said, "Do you know what I've come to say to you today?"

The group was ready. Half of the group said "Yes" and the other half said "No."

"Good. The half of you who know tell those who don't. You don't need me," said the Great Teacher. And she closed her book and left.

The community was greatly shaken. They decided they would invite the Great Teacher to come and speak one last time, for they truly believed she had something important to say. The appointed day came, and the community gathered. The Great Teacher stood before them, opened her book, and said, "Do you know what I've come to say to you today?" The room was hushed and still.

After a long silence the Great Teacher said, "Good, for now we can listen and speak and reason together."

Can you find yourself in this story? Some of us are "naysayers." We say no either because we don't think it pertains to us or because we don't think it is vital to our immediate lives. Other times we are "yea-sayers." We say yes but our yes is misdirected. We think we already know it all. We feel we have nothing left to learn. Still other times we are unwilling to do the hard work and so we remain divided. Unwilling

---

* *The Story of the Great Teacher* is a parable shared with the author by a brother from Africa.

to commit, we choose not to take a stand. But when, as a community, we are willing to sit in the silence, the Holy Spirit is freed to flow and work through us. Through God's Spirit we can become the light of discovery for one another.

This program does not follow a traditional student-teacher approach. Instead, it relies heavily upon group interaction and sharing stories. Some activities will require that we reflect on our present lives or recover old memories. Other sessions will push us to reassess our priorities. In the end we will have the opportunity to name, claim, and begin to use our gifts in unique ways. Most important, we will better understand how we can find God's will for our lives. With intentionality, we can begin to live and serve in new ways.

As we study the gifts of the Holy Spirit, we are reminded of the need to "listen and speak and reason together." As we listen, learn, and discern in community we become teachers of one another. Guided by the Holy Spirit, we learn together the ways God is working God's will in our individual and corporate lives. The process of naming, claiming, and using our gifts is a process that continues throughout our life journeys. This study is only the beginning of that journey. As we reason together, we all, individuals and community, grow as disciples of Jesus Christ.

Introducing "Many Gifts, One Spirit"

 *Participant's Workbook* pages 12-13.
"Many Gifts, One Spirit" is the theme song for the SpiritGifts program and is an excellent song to use at any time during the program. It is particularly suited to accompany *The Body of Christ* worksheet (*Leader's Resources* pages 132-35, *Participant's Workbook* page 71). You also may use it with *Responsive Listening Bible Study: 1 Corinthians 12:12-26* (*Leader's Resources* pages 128-31, *Participant's Workbook* page 69).

Songs have been used through the ages to impart images and understanding of how God works in our lives and in the world. "Many Gifts, One Spirit" is drawn from 1 Corinthians 12:4-13:

> Now there are varieties of gifts, but the same Spirit; and there are varieties of services, but the same Lord; and there are varieties of activities, but it is the same God who activates all of them in everyone.
>
> 1 CORINTHIANS 12:4-6

Let's sing this song together and learn about the many gifts that are bestowed by the one Spirit.

 After singing the song, ask participants what insights they may have gained. Possible responses:
• God is God of all people in all nations.
• The great diversity of our gifts is a blessing from God.
• God's Spirit is still creating, even today.

Many Gifts, One Spirit

1. God of change and glo-ry, God of time and space,
   when we fear the fu-ture, give to us your grace.
   In the midst of chang-ing ways give us still the grace to praise.

2. God of man-y col-ors, God of man-y signs,
   you have made us dif-ferent, bless-ing man-y kinds.
   As the old ways dis-ap-pear, let your love cast out our fear.

3. Fresh-ness of the morn-ing, new-ness of each night,
   you are still cre-at-ing end-less love and light.
   This we see, as shad-ows part, man-y gifts from one great heart.

WORDS: Al Carmines, 1973
MUSIC: Al Carmines, 1973
© 1974 Al Carmines

KATHERINE
65.65.77

Are These the Questions You Are Asking?

☞ *Participant's Workbook* page 14.

- What is God's will for my life?
- How can I know God's purpose for my life?
- How can I find fulfillment in God's world?

If these are the questions you are asking, then you're in the right place.

All of us want to live within God's purpose for our lives, for we know that when we are living within God's will, we have a peace and centeredness that we cannot find otherwise. Yet some of us have floundered around for years, unsure of what God's will is for our lives. Others of us have met with difficulty as we have pursued God's purpose that would bring us joy and completeness.

SpiritGifts will help you find answers to these questions. God's will is not defined only by the things we do or the ministries we undertake. Rather, God's will is found in our relationship with God and our relationships with other people. Simply put, living in God's will is living in tune with the heart and purposes of God. In this relationship of "God-us-others," we form a gifted community. In Christian community we are enabled to name one another's gifts and to support the use of those gifts. God gives gifts to each one of us. The Holy Spirit frees us to discern our own gifts. We also help one another to discern gifts. We recognize that these gifts are from God and are to be used for God's purposes.

The Bible says that it is because of God's grace and love—not anything we do—that we have been given gifts. Some of these gifts are named in the passage from Ephesians printed on your worksheet.

Underline the five gifts named in this passage (apostles, prophets, evangelists, pastors, teachers).

☞ Pause here.

This passage also tells why we've been given our gifts: to equip the saints (us) for the work of ministry.

Are These the Questions You Are Asking?

★ What is God's will for my life?
★ How can I know God's purpose for my life?
★ How can I find fulfillment in God's world?

These important questions are for us to answer. When we name and claim our gifts, we can make intentional choices that will align us with what God would have us do and be. As we discover our spiritual gifts, God's will in our lives is also made clear.

It is by God's grace and love—not by anything we do—that we have been given gifts.

Underline five gifts named in the passage below.

> Each of us was given grace according to the measure of Christ's gift. Therefore it is said,
> "When he ascended on high he made captivity itself a captive;
> he gave gifts to his people."
> . . . The gifts he gave were that some would be apostles, some prophets, some evangelists, some pastors and teachers, to equip the saints for the work of ministry, for building up the body of Christ, until all of us come to the unity of the faith and of the knowledge of the Son of God, to maturity, to the measure of the full stature of Christ.
>
> EPHESIANS 4:7-8, 11-13

We've been given our gifts to _____

_____

_____.

14

Other Questions to Consider

☞ *Participant's Workbook* page 15.
Have participants complete their worksheets; then continue.

I may not have all the answers to the questions you bring with you, and that's OK. There are no wrong or stupid questions. This is a learning experience for all of us. We will share our wisdom as we search for answers. There is a wisdom that comes only as we open ourselves and the Scriptures to the work of the Holy Spirit in the context of community. Like the community and the Great Teacher in the opening story, we will listen and speak and reason together.

☞ Ask participants to share their questions with the group. List them on a flip chart, chalkboard, or overhead transparency. Record the participants' exact words as much as possible. You may need to paraphrase and shorten some questions, but check with the participants to make sure they agree with any changes you make. Whatever recording method you use, keep this list for the end of the program. At the final session, use the list to see if the questions have been addressed to the participants' satisfaction. If not, they may wish to do further study.

We will refer to this list of questions at the end of the program so that we can seek answers to any questions that have not been covered to your satisfaction.

Other Questions to Consider

* ★ What are the gifts of the Holy Spirit?
* ★ Are these gifts real?
* ★ Are they biblically based?
* ★ Do they make sense in light of what I already understand about God?
* ★ Why do I need to know and study these gifts?
* ★ How do I know if I have a gift of the Spirit?
* ★ Once I discover my gifts, how do I use them?
* ★ Are gifts different from talents?
* ★ Are the gifts of the Spirit and the fruit of the Spirit the same?

These are questions we will be exploring together.
Do you have other questions?
Write them here.

15

The Work of the Spirit Within You

It is important in your spiritual journey to be in touch with the work of God's Spirit within you. To live by the Spirit is to open yourself to God's work in your life. This sacred presence empowers you to live in harmony with yourself and at peace with the world. When you live in Spirit-centered ways, you are a person of light to your family and friends. You are a sign of hope to all who come in contact with you. But when you fail to be in touch with God's spiritual work and ways in your life, your path becomes skewed, preventing you from being a vehicle through which God's love can touch others.

Although SpiritGifts is a helpful beginning, discerning God's will and getting in touch with the work of the Spirit is an ongoing process. Prayer is a key part of that continual transformation. Take time to pray. In time you set aside for prayer, wait quietly in God's presence. Know that God draws you to the places you need to be. Where do you feel the pull of your heartstrings? It always takes time to discern God's will and work for our lives. As you work out God's plan for your life, trust that day by day the Holy Spirit will guide you.

At first you will need to walk by faith as you search and seek the gifts God has given you. The walk may not feel natural in the beginning. Living in faith means doing the best that you can for who you are at that time, in that place, and trusting the rest to God. When we walk by faith we joyously awaken each day—perhaps not knowing what the day will bring, but always knowing who holds today and tomorrow: God.

As you begin to study the gifts of the Spirit and consider them according to what you know and understand about yourself, you may find you were mistaken about some of your first urgings. This is OK. Accept your humanness and go on. As you work through the SpiritGifts process with others, you can revise your judgments. You will see other ways God is working in your life. This program is not a solitary process but a communal one. Therefore, you will not need to rest solely upon your own judgments. You will have companions on the journey to help you see more clearly.

Let's look at what the Bible has to say about the work of the Holy Spirit through the ages.

☞ Display overhead, page 54.
Participant's Workbook pages 16-17.
Call on a participant to read the first scripture. Then read the response, instructing the participants to fill in their worksheets. Continue in this manner to complete the worksheet.

Then afterward I will pour out my spirit on all flesh; your sons and your daughters shall prophesy, your old men shall dream dreams, and your young men shall see visions. Even on the male and female slaves, in those days, I will pour out my spirit.

JOEL 2:28-29

The Holy Spirit has been a promise of God to you since the time of the writings of the prophet Joel in the Hebrew Scriptures.

Just as Jesus acted through the guidance and empowerment of the Holy Spirit, so can you.

> "I baptize you with water for repentance, but one who is more powerful than I is coming after me; I am not worthy to carry his sandals. He will baptize you with the Holy Spirit and fire."
>
> MATTHEW 3:11

> "But you will receive power when the Holy Spirit has come upon you; and you will be my witnesses in Jerusalem, in all Judea and Samaria, and to the ends of the earth."
>
> ACTS 1:8

And just as the Holy Spirit led the first disciples through the events of Pentecost and into the first struggling days of the church's history, so you will be led and strengthened.

On the day of Pentecost and throughout Christian history we have seen how the Holy Spirit works to bring about God's purposes on earth. We also see how wrong we can go, as individuals and as the church, when acting out of our own selfish, ego-centered wills instead of acting in Spirit-led ways.

There are many lessons to be learned about the Holy Spirit—about how the Spirit works and is taught in Scripture. SpiritGifts concentrates on how the Holy Spirit empowers and equips us for the work of ministry within the Christian community—all of this so the reign of God will come as God plans.

So as you continue this SpiritGifts journey, remember to do so in an attitude of prayer. Remember not only to call upon but also to rely upon God's presence working in your life. As your life and work are intertwined and directed by the guidance of the Holy Spirit, you will be attuned to God's will. You will know God's purpose for your life as a part of God's community.

The Work of the Spirit Within You

The Holy Spirit has been a promise of God to you since the time of the writings of the prophet Joel in the Hebrew Scriptures.

Just as *Jesus* acted through the guidance and empowerment of the Holy Spirit, so can you.

And just as the Holy Spirit led *the first disciples* through the events of Pentecost and into the first struggling days of the church's history, so you will be led and strengthened.

———

The Holy Spirit works to bring about *God's purposes on earth*.

The Holy Spirit *empowers* and *equips* us for the work of ministry within the Christian community.

The Work of the Spirit Within You

> Then afterward
>   I will pour out my spirit on all flesh;
> your sons and your daughters shall prophesy,
>   your old men shall dream dreams,
>   and your young men shall see visions.
> Even on the male and female slaves,
>   in those days, I will pour out my spirit.
>
> JOEL 2:28-29

_____ has been a promise of God to you since the time of the writings of the prophet Joel in the Hebrew Scriptures.

> "I baptize you with water for repentance, but one who is more powerful than I is coming after me; I am not worthy to carry his sandals. He will baptize you with the Holy Spirit and fire."
>
> MATTHEW 3:11

Just as _____ acted through the guidance and empowerment of the Holy Spirit, so can you.

> "But you will receive power when the Holy Spirit has come upon you; and you will be my witnesses in Jerusalem, in all Judea and Samaria, and to the ends of the earth."
>
> ACTS 1:8

And just as the Holy Spirit led _____

16

_____ through the event of Pentecost and into the first struggling days of the church's history, so you will be led and strengthened.

* * * *

The Holy Spirit works to bring about _____

_____ .

The Holy Spirit _____ and

_____ us for the work of ministry within the Christian community.

17

The Bible and Spiritual Gifts

SpiritGifts bases its study of spiritual gifts on four principal passages from the letters of Paul: Romans 12:3-8; 1 Corinthians 12:4-11; 1 Corinthians 12:27-31; and Ephesians 4:7-16. In each case, Paul identifies the gifts by name. For example, in Romans he writes:

> We have gifts that differ according to the grace given to us: *prophecy,* in proportion to faith; *ministry,* in ministering; the *teacher,* in teaching. . . .
>
> ROMANS 12:6-7

Likewise, in 1 Corinthians he writes:

> Now concerning spiritual gifts, brothers and sisters, I do not want you to be uninformed. . . . To one is given through the Spirit the utterance of *wisdom,* and to another the utterance of *knowledge.* . . .
>
> 1 CORINTHIANS 12:1, 8

And in Ephesians he writes:

> The gifts he gave were that some would be *apostles,* some *prophets,* some *evangelists.* . . .
>
> EPHESIANS 4:11

Some of the gifts are repeated in more than one verse and more than one text.

In each letter Paul is concerned directly or indirectly with doctrinal and ethical problems that were disturbing the Gentile churches of the Greco-Roman world: Rome, Corinth, and Ephesus. He writes about God's eternal purpose for God's people, as well as the glorious entitlements and duties of all believers. The gifts bestowed by the Holy Spirit vividly demonstrate the wondrous privilege of being a follower of Christ, even as they are a call to Christian responsibility.

☞ *Participant's Workbook* page 18.

This chart shows the gifts identified by Paul in each text, as well as the names used for the gifts in this program. Other resources name gifts that are not included here, such as hospitality and humor. Paul admonishes persons to "extend hospitality" in Romans 12:13, but nowhere does he state that this is a gift of the Spirit. Likewise, although there are examples of biblical quips employed by Christ, nowhere in the Bible is it stated that humor is a spiritual gift. The eighteen spiritual gifts identified here are those most commonly recognized by veterans of spiritual gifts studies.

Some resources omit gifts such as tongues, interpretation, and miracles. Why? Some people are fearful that acknowledging these gifts will cause division. Others acknowledge that these gifts are not commonly manifested by the Spirit or are not part of their particular religious culture. However, in most instances, all eighteen gifts can be seen in larger bodies of Christians coming from diverse backgrounds. SpiritGifts includes all eighteen, recognizing that most students of spiritual gifts are eager and willing to struggle with the questions.

Now take a few minutes to find these four passages in your Bible translation. Underline the gifts with a pencil or pen as you identify them.

> ☞ Note: The gift of ministry found in the passage from Romans comes from the Greek word for deacon, *diakovia*, meaning service. Therefore, this gift also could be listed with the gift of assisting. However, because the early church used deacon as a pastoring office of the church, it is listed here with the gift of pastoring.

The Bible and Spiritual Gifts

In SpiritGifts the gift is called . . .	Romans 12:3-8	1 Corinthians 12:4-11	1 Corinthians 12:27-31	Ephesians 4:7-16
Prophecy	prophecy	prophecy	prophets	prophets
Pastoring	ministry			pastors
Teaching	teacher		teachers	teachers
Encouragement	exhorter			
Giving	giver			
Compassion	compassionate			
Wisdom		wisdom		
Knowledge		knowledge		
Faith		faith		
Healing		healing	healing	
Miracles		miracles	power/ miracles	
Discernment		discernment		
Tongues		tongues	tongues	
Interpretation		interpretation	interpret	
Apostleship			apostles	apostles
Assisting			assistance	
Leadership	leader		leadership	
Evangelism				evangelists

Find these four scripture passages in your Bible translation. Underline the gifts with a pencil or pen as you identify them.

18

An Introduction to Responsive Listening Bible Study

Bible study is an important and consistent component of SpiritGifts. It lays the foundation for each step of the group's process. Throughout the program, we will be using the Responsive Listening Bible Study method. This method helps us open ourselves to hear God's word anew and apply it to our hearts and lives. It allows us to gain insights and hear God's voice through the reflections of others as Bible passages and stories meet us in our own life stories.

☞ *Participant's Workbook* pages 19-20.

This small group Bible study method and variations on it have been used throughout many parts of the world. The particular version outlined here is a variation on the Base Christian Community Method of Central America. It also has been called the African Method and the Oral Tradition Approach. Through the lens of Scripture we will be challenged to look at the present conditions of our own lives, our community, our nation, and our world. Together we will reflect on what the Bible is saying to us about our roles in each. Then we will be challenged to respond to one another and take action grounded in prayer.

☞ Invite participants to break into small groups of four to six. Have the members of each group count off. Then choose a number from one to four or one to six and announce that the person with that number is the designated facilitator of the group. Explain that the facilitator will keep time and guide the process by following the instructions on pages 19-20 of the *Participant's Workbook*.

Read through the self-explanatory directions step-by-step with the participants. Remind them that this method is different from a discussion Bible study. Ask if there are any questions. Tell them that this method will take twenty-five to thirty minutes, and that you will tell them when five minutes remain. At that point they should move to step 8, prayer time, if they have not yet done so. If a group finishes ahead of time, they may remain silent and pray for those groups who are still sharing.

Proceed to *Responsive Listening Bible Study: Ephesians 4:1-16 (Leader's Resources* pages 63-66, *Participant's Workbook* pages 21-22).

NOTE: An alternative method of Bible study for reluctant groups is to read the text through one time and then move through the following three steps:
1. Discuss: What is the main thought or theme of this passage?
2. Share: How does this information add to your understanding of the gifts of the Holy Spirit?
3. Facilitator shares a closing prayer for the entire group.

Responsive Listening Bible Study
(Eight Steps)

STEP 1. Read the passage slowly, with one person reading out loud. [3-4 minutes]

STEP 2. In silence, recall the word or phrase that most caught your attention and reflect on this word. [1 minute]

STEP 3. Each person shares the word or phrase with the group without comment. [1-2 minutes]

STEP 4. A different person reads the passage out loud again. [3-4 minutes]

STEP 5. Think out: "Where does this passage touch my life or our community or our nation or our world today?" Each person responds using an "I" statement (not "The church thinks . . ." or "The world thinks . . ." but "I think . . ."). [3-5 minutes]

STEP 6. A different person reads the passage out loud again. [3-4 minutes]

STEP 7. Think out: "From what I have heard and shared, what does God want me to do or be this week? How does God invite me to change?" Each person responds using an "I" statement. Share as time allows, making sure to leave time for prayer (step 8). You may want to jot down a few notes as the person on your right is speaking, so that you will remember what to pray about in step 8. [3-5 minutes]

STEP 8. One at a time, each person briefly prays out loud for the person on his or her right, naming what that person

19

shared in step 7. The group may wish to join hands. [3-5 minutes]

> NOTE: Be brief in steps 5 and 7. Do not elaborate, teach, or explain. Listen without responding. No one is to comment, critique, or build on what is said as if in a discussion group. If there is more than one group, remain in quiet reflection and prayer until everyone is finished.

20

Responsive Listening Bible Study

E P H E S I A N S   4 : 1 - 1 6

 Participant's Workbook pages 21-22.

This is the first of three major texts used in SpiritGifts: Ephesians 4:1-16; Romans 12:3-8; and 1 Corinthians 12:1, 4-31. Six Bible studies are provided, each using the Responsive Listening Bible Study method. The additional studies include Matthew 7:15-20 and Galatians 5:22-25; Acts 1:1-8; and 1 Corinthians 13. Depending upon the length and depth of your program, you may or may not choose to use all six studies. Encourage participants to take time at home to read and reflect on those texts that you do not study as a group.

This is the first time participants will use the Responsive Listening Bible Study method. If you have not already done so, read the introduction on page 60 and the steps outlined on pages 61-62. Answer any questions about procedure. During the study, walk from group to group, asking what step they are on and if they have any questions or concerns. Be attuned to groups who get bogged down and to facilitators who do not keep their small groups moving through the steps as described.

In the fourth chapter of Ephesians, emphasis is placed on the things that contribute to the peace, unity, and growth of the church in contrast to actions that support the powers of division and destruction. God's mysterious intention is to unite all things in heaven and earth. By the gifts of Christ, the church is equipped for ministry and service.

If you have not already divided into small groups, do so now and have the groups follow the step-by-step instructions for Responsive Listening Bible Study (*Participant's Workbook* pages 19-20, *Leader's Resources* pages 61-62).

I therefore, the prisoner in the Lord, beg you to lead a life worthy of the calling to which you have been called, with all humility and gentleness, with patience, bearing with one another in love, making every effort to maintain the unity of the Spirit in the bond of peace. There is one body and one Spirit, just as you were called to the one hope of your calling, one Lord, one faith, one baptism, one God and Father of all, who is above all and through all and in all.

But each of us was given grace according to the measure of Christ's gift. Therefore it is said,

"When he ascended on high he made captivity itself a captive; he gave gifts to his people."

(When it says, "He ascended," what does it mean but that he had also descended into the lower parts of the earth? He who descended is the same one who ascended far above all the heavens, so that he might fill all things.) The gifts he gave were that some would be apostles, some prophets, some evangelists, some pastors and teachers, to equip the saints for the work of ministry, for building up the body of Christ, until all of us come to the unity of the faith and of the knowledge of the Son of God, to maturity, to the measure of the full stature of Christ. We must no longer be children, tossed to and fro and blown about by every wind of doctrine, by people's trickery, by their craftiness in deceitful scheming. But speaking the truth in love, we must grow up in every way into him who is the head, into Christ, from whom the whole body, joined and knit together by every ligament with which it is equipped, as each part is working properly, promotes the body's growth in building itself up in love.

EPHESIANS 4:1-16

 When the groups have completed their study, they are to locate and underline the five gifts of the Spirit listed in the text. (These are underlined for you.)

Responsive Listening Bible Study

EPHESIANS 4:1-16

In the fourth chapter of Ephesians, emphasis is placed on the things that contribute to the peace, unity, and growth of the church, in contrast to actions that support the powers of division and destruction. God's mysterious intention is to unite all things in heaven and earth. By the gifts of Christ, the church is equipped for ministry and service.

I therefore, the prisoner in the Lord, beg you to lead a life worthy of the calling to which you have been called, with all humility and gentleness, with patience, bearing with one another in love, making every effort to maintain the unity of the Spirit in the bond of peace. There is one body and one Spirit, just as you were called to the one hope of your calling, one Lord, one faith, one baptism, one God and Father of all, who is above all and through all and in all.

But each of us was given grace according to the measure of Christ's gift. Therefore it is said,

"When he ascended on high he made captivity itself a captive;
he gave gifts to his people."

(When it says, "He ascended," what does it mean but that he had also descended into the lower parts of the earth? He who descended is the same one who ascended far above all the heavens, so that he might fill all things.) The gifts he gave were that some would be apostles, some prophets, some evangelists, some pastors and teachers, to equip the saints for the work of ministry, for building up the body of Christ, until all of us come to the unity of the faith and of the knowledge of the Son of God, to maturity, to the measure of the full stature of Christ. We must no longer be children, tossed to and fro and blown about by every wind of doctrine, by people's trickery, by their craftiness in deceitful scheming. But speaking the truth in love, we must grow up in every way into him who is the head, into Christ, from whom the whole body, joined and knit together by every ligament with which it is equipped, as each part is working properly, promotes the body's growth in building itself up in love.

EPHESIANS 4:1-16

21

In your small groups, follow the step-by-step instructions on pages 19-20 to study Ephesians 4:1-16.

When your group has completed the Bible study, locate and underline the five gifts of the Spirit listed in the text. When you are finished, reflect on the passage in silence and wait for further instructions.

NOTES:

22

Why Do I Need to Know and Study the Gifts of the Holy Spirit?

Display overhead, page 68.
Participant's Workbook page 23.

It is true that many people have been living a Christian life for years without knowing about the gifts of the Holy Spirit.

Every congregation has an "Aunt Gertie." You know her. She has been a member of the church for more than a hundred years. You can just hear Aunt Gertie say: "I've been a member of this congregation since I was a little girl. I've never heard anything about gifts before, so why do I need to know about them now?"

You can answer the "Aunt Gerties" you know by reminding them that God's work in our lives is not entirely contingent on our knowledge or even our agreement to work with God. God has always been at work in each one of us. But when we study, name, and claim our gifts, we can *tear down our resistance to God* and *work along with God's will for our lives.*

When we complete this program, we will be excited and want to share our newfound information with others. But we have to be careful not to be smug and think that we are taking God to them. We must remember that God is already at work in each individual we meet.

We have the wonderful opportunity to be part of God's gifted community. To every person, God gives gifts. We see these gifts evidenced through a person's abilities, talents, personality strengths, and life circumstances. The Holy Spirit leads us to see our own gifts and to recognize the gifts in others. We can help one another to be open to all of God's good gifts and to use them in the many present opportunities for ministry and mission.

We use our gifts as we are engaged in God's mission throughout the world. We use them wherever we are and with whomever we meet: in our homes, at work, in politics, in organizations and institutions, on the street, and in our congregations. We are supported in their use as other Christians recognize and name our gifts and support us in the use of those gifts.

Why Do I Need to Know and Study the Gifts of the Holy Spirit?

When we study, name, and claim our gifts, we can

★ tear down our resistance to God

★ work along with God's will for our lives

Remember: God is already at work in each individual we meet.

Why Do I Need to Know and Study the Gifts of the Holy Spirit?

It is true that many people have been living a Christian life for years without knowing about the gifts of the Holy Spirit. God's work in our lives is not entirely contingent on our knowledge or even our agreement to work with God. God has always been at work in each one of us.

But when we study, name, and claim our gifts, we can

★_____

★_____

Remember: God is already at work in each individual we meet.

23

What Is a Gift of the Holy Spirit?

☞ Display overhead, page 72.
Participant's Workbook page 24.

Instruct the participants to complete their worksheets as you present the following information.

A gift of the Holy Spirit is

★ a *"grace gift"*; it is not something we can *earn or attain* on our own

A person, by her or his very nature, is a gift of God. Our Creator has given us everything we need to fulfill our own destiny, according to God's will, and to be who God plans for us to be. God intends for us to be gifts of grace to the world.

★ *designed* and *designated* by God

We need to remember that our destiny is not an immutable fate forced upon us by a divinity without a heart. Instead, we work with God as we cocreate our lives. Our gifts bring us into covenant relationship with God and our community.

★ used for the *whole Christian community*

We are responsible for using our gifts in the church and the world. When we name our gifts and take responsibility in the area of each of our gifts, those who confirm us also recognize our authority. They understand each gift as an articulation of our lives. As we live out our gifts, we commit ourselves to living in covenant relationship with other believers and use our gifts for the good of all. In practical terms, our gifts require responsibility and sacrifice.

★ energized by the *Holy Spirit*

That same Spirit gives us the responsibility of investing our gifts with God in the continuing healing of the world. Each one of us has something to give that no one else can give. We open ourselves to be creative and to live in the unexpected. We set aside our own judgment of our work and our perfectionism that inhibits us. We dive in knowing that all new endeavors will not succeed, and that's okay. Or as a bumper sticker reads: "Anything worth doing is worth doing badly." The Spirit frees us to be our best creative self.

★ used in obedience to *God's will*

A primary responsibility of the church is to help evoke the gifts within us and then hold us accountable so that we can experience the joys of both giving and receiving. When we become aware of our own gifts and give attention to using them, we have the experience of growing toward wholeness. We are working out God's chosen purpose for our lives.

★ for the healing of *all of God's creation*

Our gifts carry us into the world and make us participants with God in life. If we take our gifts seriously, they will set off a transformation—not only within ourselves but also within our congregations—that will bring in a whole new age of the Spirit. Gifted people live and interact differently—not only with other people, but also with all of God's creation.

What Is a Gift of the Holy Spirit?

A gift of the Holy Spirit is

★ a *"grace gift"*; it is not something we can *earn or attain* on our own
★ *designed* and *designated* by God
★ used for the *whole Christian community*
★ energized by the *Holy Spirit*
★ used in obedience to *God's will*
★ for the healing of *all of God's creation*

What Is A Gift of the Holy Spirit?

A gift of the Holy Spirit is

★ a _____; it is not something

we can _____ on our own

★ _____ and _____

by God

★ used for the _____

★ energized by the _____

★ used in obedience to _____

★ for the healing of _____

_____

24

How Can I Search Out My Gifts?

Display overhead, page 75.
Participant's Workbook page 25.
Instruct the participants to complete their worksheets as you present the following information.

How do we go about discerning and naming the gifts that the Holy Spirit has set upon us? Here are three steps to guide you.

1. Prayerfully Study the Gifts.

Open yourself to God's will as you seek God's purpose in your life. Ask God to free you to hear the inner voice of the Holy Spirit and the voices of other companions on the journey. Study the meaning of each gift so that you will be able to recognize it when you see it in yourself or another person. The bestowing and use of a gift may be lived out in quiet, simple ways. Or a gift may be lived in flamboyant ways, easily distinguished.

2. Be Open to Find All Your Gifts.

You probably have more than one gift, so study all of them. By exposing yourself to various ministries, you may find a gift that you did not realize you had. The first time you try something new you may feel hesitant, but with each try you could find greater comfort and possibly a "home." Willingness to try something new may uncover a gift you never knew you possessed.

There are some *clues* you may want to look for as you study the gifts. Sometimes people feel some hesitancy toward a gift due to old stereotypes that the gift carries. For example, you might be reluctant to study the gift of evangelism if you equate the gift with negative past experiences such as holier-than-thou attitudes. A second clue is to pay attention to those things you find yourself griping about at church or in your work in the community. Perhaps this nagging issue has your attention for a reason. That reason may lead you to a specific gift to meet a pressing ministry need in your congregation or community.

3. Name Your Gifts.

As you discern and name your gifts, let others know. In this way you can take your rightful place in the work of all believers. It is our responsibility to name and claim our gifts. To fail to do so is to fail to serve within the church community as Christ intended. There may be times during this program when you think you have a gift, but you are not quite sure. As you test your gifts within the context of doing ministry, you will find the confidence to name and use your gifts. Is the gift well grounded in the community of faith and relevant in the context of your congregation's ministry? You'll want to validate your gifts with your faith community, small group, or spiritual mentor. This means finding persons to talk to who are discovering and working within their spiritual gifts and who can help you to clarify your gifts.

How Can I Search Out My Gifts?

How do we go about discerning and naming the gifts that the Holy Spirit has set upon us?

1. Prayerfully study the gifts.

2. Be open to find all your gifts.

3. Name your gifts.

How Can I Search Out My Gifts?

How do we go about discerning and naming the gifts that the Holy Spirit has set upon us? Here are three steps to guide you.

1. _____

2. _____

3. _____

25

God Is Always with Me

Recognizing how God breaks into our routine lives is important groundwork in the search to name and claim our spiritual gifts. We need to become aware of the times and places God is working through our gifts to bring about good in our lives for the greater community.

God is always with us. Some of us feel this assurance most when life is running smoothly and evenly. Others are assured of God's presence in times of trouble or stress. Still others are aware of the nearness of God during the high moments of life.

Susan is one person who knows God's presence in her life. Susan runs a hectic schedule with a full household and a full-time job. Sometimes women and men avoid God by frantically rushing from one activity to another, but not Susan. On weekends Susan enjoys working in her herb garden. "Getting down and getting dirty" is just what she needs to move into quieter space and get in touch with the Center of Life. In the "ordinary times" Susan is most aware of God's presence.

Jim also knows God's presence in his life, but in a different way. Jim buried his wife last spring. In his deepest grief, he knew God was present. Surrounded by Christian friends, he knew he was not alone. In prayer he called upon God for the Divine's sustaining power so he could go on. Now when loneliness threatens to overtake him, he reflects on those moments to find spiritual strength for the day.

Participant's Workbook page 26.

If you are leading a retreat or if time allows, invite participants to take plenty of time to reflect on this activity. Otherwise, set a time limit for the activity. Have each person find a partner and discuss. Call everyone together at the end of the allotted time and ask each person to briefly share one of his or her own life experiences.

God Is Always with Me

List one to five events in your life in which you have felt God's presence. These are times when you have felt God very near and close to you. They may have been spiritual mountaintop highs or simply ordinary times in your life.

1. _____

2. _____

3. _____

4. _____

5. _____

How have you seen God's faithfulness as you look back at your life? Do you sense any pattern or common thread in God's revealing presence? As you discern your gifts during SpiritGifts, how might you know that God is revealing them to you? What clues, if any, have you uncovered?

Find a partner and discuss.

NOTES:

26

LEADER

Gifts and God's Will

☞ Display overhead, page 81.
Participant's Workbook page 27.
You may wish to have participants take turns reading this out loud. Read each heading and then ask for a volunteer to read out loud. Instruct the participants to complete their worksheets as you move through the material.

1. Each One of Us Has Been Given *Gifts*.

Each one of us has been given gifts by the Holy Spirit. We can use these gifts to live in peace with God's purpose for our lives. We can employ these gifts to take our place and be an active part in God's wonderful plan for the world. Our choice is simple. We have the wonderful invitation to be a part of God's work in reconciling and reuniting the world. When we work toward that cause, we are God's people.

2. You Have *Particular Gifts* as a Unique Child of God.

God wants you to use your gifts to live God's plan for your life. Your gifts are unique. Because you have particular gifts as a unique child of God, your gifts influence the specific ways in which you respond to God's call in your life. Your gifts shape the way you live your life.

3. Using Your Spiritual Gifts Brings You *Joy!*

How can the gifts of the Holy Spirit within you bring you deep joy? As you see and live within the gifts of God, you have a sense of doing what you were created to do and of being who you were created to be. You affirm your best self, as God planned for you to be. You find satisfaction and happiness as you do particular things well. You act on your values and beliefs. You see your deepest longings and hopes fulfilled as you use your gifts effectively to achieve realistic goals. God may ask you to stretch your potential, but God will not ask you to do things that are not true to who you are. Remember that each one of the gifts can be lived out in a number of ways.

4. Reaching Your *Full Potential* Is God's Plan.

As you use your gifts, you begin to understand that reaching your potential is more important than reaching the goal or goals you have set. If you are successful by the world's standards but are unfaithful to what is true and right and of God, then you fail in your efforts as a disciple.

As you discern and use your gifts, you enter an exciting experience of self-discovery. You find new opportunities to use the full potential of your life. It is exciting to know that you can be a part of God's plan to renew the world!

What are the thoughts and examples that come to mind when you think of "God's plan to renew the world"?

☞ List these and other possible responses on a flip chart or chalkboard:
- Helping to build a Habitat for Humanity house in your community.
- Teaching children, through word and example, about God's love for them.
- Sharing a meal and spiritual conversation with someone who needs food.

Gifts and God's Will

1. Each one of us has been given *gifts.*

2. You have *particular gifts* as a unique child of God.

3. Using your spiritual gifts brings you *joy!*

4. Reaching your *full potential* is God's plan.

Gifts and God's Will

1. Each one of us has been given _____.

Each one of us has been given gifts by the Holy Spirit. We can use these gifts to live in peace with God's purpose for our lives. We can employ these gifts to take our place and be an active part in God's wonderful plan for the world. Our choice is simple. We have the wonderful invitation to be a part of God's work in reconciling and reuniting the world. When we work toward that cause, we are God's people.

2. You have _____ as a unique child of God.

God wants you to use your gifts to live God's plan for your life. Your gifts are unique. Because you have particular gifts as a unique child of God, your gifts influence the specific ways in which you respond to God's call in your life. Your gifts shape the way you live your life.

3. Using your spiritual gifts brings you _____!

How can the gifts of the Holy Spirit within you bring you deep joy? As you use and live within the gifts of God, you have a sense of doing what you were created to do and of being who you were created to be. You affirm your best self, as God planned for you to be. You find satisfaction and happiness as you do particular things well. You act on your values and beliefs. You see your deepest longings and hopes fulfilled as you use your gifts effectively to achieve realistic goals. God may ask you to stretch your potential,

27

but God will not ask you to do things that are not true to who you are. Remember that each one of the gifts can be lived out in a number of ways.

4. Reaching your _____ is God's plan.

As you use your gifts, you begin to understand that reaching your potential is more important than reaching the goal or goals you have set. If you are successful by the world's standards but are unfaithful to what is true and right and of God, then you fail in your efforts as a disciple.

As you discern and use your gifts, you enter an exciting experience of self-discovery. You find new opportunities to use the full potential of your life. It is exciting to know that you can be a part of God's plan to renew the world!

28

When I Live in God's Will

 Participant's Workbook page 29.
Have the participants complete their worksheets as you present the material.

1. When I live in God's will, *I Know What to Put First in My Life.*

When we function according to the gifts we know God has given us, we stop trying to swim up stream. We can't do everything. Knowing our gifts helps us to know where to place our time and energy. We begin to prioritize our tasks and jobs, no longer overcome by the thought that everything is of equal importance to serve God and the community.

2. When I live in God's will, *I Am Free to Say "No" and to Say "Yes."*

It is hard for some of us to say "no" when we are asked to do something worthy. We take it as a compliment when others come to us with a job that needs to be undertaken, and we do not want to disappoint them. Nor do we want them to think we are not willing participants in the work of the faith community. Oftentimes there are many reasons we should say "no" when we say "yes." Identifying our gifts and telling others what our gifts are helps us to say "no." In this way we can have the time and resources free to say "yes" when we can contribute our very best.

3. When I live in God's will, *Burnout Is Negligible.*

We all "burn out" when we give energy to jobs and tasks that just don't fit our gifts. When we name and claim our gifts and then agree to do the tasks and jobs that fall under those gifts, we feel revitalized and energized to do the work and more. Of course, if we overwork our gifts and don't take care of ourselves, burnout can still result. Feelings of anger and resentment serve as warning signs of overextension. Symptoms of insomnia, frantic business, or an out-of-control calendar are all signals leading toward burnout.

4. When I live in God's will, *My Self-Esteem Is Lifted.*

When we accomplish a task or project that we know God has called and equipped us to do, we feel good about the work and ourselves. Our self-esteem is lifted, and we find pleasure in the dignity of our work, the elegance of its simplicity, and the essential responsibility in serving others. Using our gifts in ways that free us and others to be our best selves helps us find creative ways to express our love for Jesus Christ.

Some of us find it hard to accept that God has truly gifted us. We affirm gifts in others but not in ourselves. We may find it easier to hide behind false humility than to take responsibility to name and claim our gifts. This is why we identify our gifts in community with others. Companions on the journey aid us in being honest and realistic about our gifts. We find a mutuality where we are accountable for the gifts God has given us. The congregation nurtures and forms us. They educate us and help us grow. Finally they send us into mission.

When I Live in God's Will

1. When I live in God's will, *I know what to put first in my life.*

2. When I live in God's will, *I am free to say "no" and to say "yes."*

3. When I live in God's will, *burnout is negligible.*

4. When I live in God's will, *my self-esteem is lifted.*

When I Live in God's Will

1. When I live in God's will, _____

_____.

Knowing our gifts helps us to know where to place our time and energy. We begin to prioritize our tasks and jobs, no longer overcome by the thought that everything is of equal importance to serve God and the community.

2. When I live in God's will, _____

_____.

Identifying our gifts and telling others what our gifts are help us to say "no." In this way we can have the time and resources free to say "yes" when we can contribute our very best.

3. When I live in God's will, _____

_____.

When we name and claim our gifts and then agree to do the tasks and jobs that fall under those gifts, we feel revitalized and energized to do the work and more. Of course, if we overwork our gifts and don't take care of ourselves, burnout can still result.

4. When I live in God's will, _____

_____.

When we accomplish a task or project that we know God has called and equipped us to do, we feel good about the work and ourselves. Our self-esteem is lifted, and we find pleasure in the dignity of our work, the elegance of its simplicity, and the essential responsibility in serving others.

29

Spiritual Gifts Survey

☞ *Participant's Workbook* pages 30-34.

A personal survey is one tool for discovering and discerning your gifts. It is not the only tool, nor is it the most helpful tool for everyone. The survey is one of many activities SpiritGifts employs and does not carry more weight than other exercises in the program.

The survey precedes more in-depth Bible study and specific descriptions of the gifts so that your responses to the statements are spontaneous and unbiased by additional information about the gifts. The survey also serves to give you a quick overview of all eighteen gifts of the Spirit, helping you begin to look at the gifts in a personal light. Remember that your first inclination may not be your strongest gift.

The statements are not explained in detail. If you do not understand a statement, give the best answer you can according to what you think it means. You may choose not to respond to a particular statement and move on to the next. If the statement is not applicable, enter a zero in the numbered answer space.

☞ Allow ten to fifteen minutes for participants to complete the survey. If they need more time than this, they are pausing for too much reflection. Remind them that they are to record their initial, spontaneous responses.

Participant's Workbook page 35.

Have participants transfer their responses to the *Spiritual Gifts Survey Answer Sheet* and follow the instructions provided.

Participant's Workbook page 36.

After everyone has completed an answer sheet, have the participants list their top three gifts according to the highest numerical values. Allow them to select a fourth gift—any gift of their choosing—and write it in the designated space for later referral.

Participant's Workbook pages 37-41.

Now have everyone turn to the descriptions of the gifts. As you name each gift aloud, have the participants who listed that gift as one of their top three gifts raise their hands. Ask one of these persons to read the description aloud. If no one has listed a particular gift, you may read the description aloud. Continue until all of the descriptions have been read.

Spiritual Gifts Survey

Rank each of the following statements as it applies to your experience or inclination.

Much (3), Some (2), Little (1), or None (0).

This is a self survey, not a test. There are no right or wrong answers. Therefore, be sure to let your responses reflect your opinions of yourself. This survey will not be shared except as you choose.

_____ 1. I make a point to be with people of other cultures and ethnic backgrounds.

_____ 2. I see destructive patterns in people's lives and help them to find healthier ways of living.

_____ 3. I listen as other people tell me about their religious experiences and spiritual journeys.

_____ 4. People often seek me out and ask me to pray with them.

_____ 5. I can explain in simple ways complex ideas about God and how to live as a disciple.

_____ 6. I often praise coworkers for their good work and attitudes.

_____ 7. I carefully get all the information I need before moving into action.

_____ 8. I can share deep truths with others about their problems.

_____ 9. When I see a need, I spring to action and do something about it.

30

Much (3), Some (2), Little (1), or None (0).

____ 10. I am materially blessed, and I give what I can to others freely.

____ 11. Being in charge doesn't mean I have to control everything.

____ 12. I can sit and simply listen to someone who needs a listening ear.

____ 13. I do the best I can and leave the rest in God's hands.

____ 14. I speak up and tell others when I don't believe they are telling the whole truth.

____ 15. I have experienced times when something miraculously happened that was contrary to natural law.

____ 16. I look for opportunities to bring hope and God's comfort to those who are sick.

____ 17. I have spoken in verbal utterances that praise God but are not understandable by human ears.

____ 18. I have been able to learn foreign languages easily.

____ 19. My circle of friends looks like a meeting of the United Nations.

____ 20. I am energized when I speak about what needs to be changed in church and other arenas.

____ 21. Inviting others to join me in something I enjoy is something I do every week.

____ 22. I find myself time and again listening to people's spiritual struggles and offering guidance.

31

Much (3), Some (2), Little (1), or None (0).

_____ 23. When I am a student in a class or the teacher of a class, other participants are energized and motivated.

_____ 24. I am able to work with people and help them do their best.

_____ 25. I am able to grasp deep truths about God and make sense of them.

_____ 26. I am able to use my knowledge in complex situations, weighing the pros and cons, and know what is right.

_____ 27. I don't mind lending a hand and doing the trivial jobs that are often overlooked.

_____ 28. I give 10 percent of my income and more to my church and other charitable needs.

_____ 29. When I am working on a group project, I make the extra effort to communicate with everyone.

_____ 30. Stopping what I am doing to help someone in need is a normal part of my day.

_____ 31. When I believe that something is of God, I act boldly on my belief.

_____ 32. My friends often ask me to help sort out what is real and what is phony.

_____ 33. God has mysteriously intervened in extraordinary ways in my presence.

_____ 34. I am able to counsel others to help restore them to mental and spiritual health.

32

Much (3), Some (2), Little (1), or None (0).

_____ 35. I have spoken in a language that I am not normally able to speak.

_____ 36. I can hear verbal sounds not understood by others and understand what is meant.

_____ 37. I rejoice that our church has such a wide diversity of people.

_____ 38. I can see change coming and am not afraid to help people make the needed changes.

_____ 39. Sharing how I became a Christian comes naturally for me.

_____ 40. I can be called upon when someone needs help in making difficult decisions.

_____ 41. I am good at giving directions to people so that they can complete projects successfully.

_____ 42. I make a point to say a kind word to those whose abilities I admire.

_____ 43. I am deeply satisfied when I study in order to explain hard concepts to others.

_____ 44. I don't panic in difficult situations, but weigh all the circumstances to find a solution.

_____ 45. I'd rather stay in the background doing the labor than be out front speaking or teaching.

_____ 46. I spend a lot of time earning and raising money and an equal amount of time giving it away.

33

Much (3), Some (2), Little (1), or None (0).

____ 47. I am good at organizing and leading a group to meet their goals.

____ 48. I walk gently with people who are grieving, and can walk with them in their process of healing.

____ 49. I live the best I can each day, one day at a time, not worrying about tomorrow.

____ 50. I can "see through" people and circumstances and know what is real and what is not.

____ 51. Time and again I have seen miracles, acts contrary to natural law, occur.

____ 52. I am able to help, comfort, and counsel when people are deeply troubled.

____ 53. I have had the experience of "speaking in tongues."

____ 54. I am able to move into another culture, speak another language, and feel at home.

34

Spiritual Gifts Survey Answer Sheet

Transfer your responses from the survey to this answer sheet. Add the total at the end of each line. Remember, this survey reflects only your past history and not what God may be doing even now in this moment or will do in your future.

Gift	Responses			Total
APOSTLESHIP	1	19	37	
PROPHECY	2	20	38	
EVANGELISM	3	21	39	
PASTORING	4	22	40	
TEACHING	5	23	41	
ENCOURAGEMENT	6	24	42	
KNOWLEDGE	7	25	43	
WISDOM	8	26	44	
ASSISTING	9	27	45	
GIVING	10	28	46	
LEADERSHIP	11	29	47	
COMPASSION	12	30	48	
FAITH	13	31	49	
DISCERNMENT	14	32	50	
MIRACLES	15	33	51	
HEALING	16	34	52	
TONGUES	17	35	53	
INTERPRETATION	18	36	54	

35

My Top Three Gifts

List your top three gifts in the order of highest numerical value as indicated by the survey sheet. **Please list only three.**

First

_____

Second

_____

Third

_____

List one more gift that you sense may be yours

_____

Now proceed to page 37. Begin reading about the gifts that may be yours.

36

Gifts of the Spirit: Descriptions

The gifts are divided into three categories: gifts of word, gifts of deed, and gifts of sign. This reminds us that we are disciples who live the ways of Christ in

what we say (**word**),
what we do (**deed**),
ways and signs that point to God (**sign**).

Division between the categories of word, deed, and sign are not always clear-cut. A person may live out a gift in one, two, or all three of these ways. For instance, a woman with the gift of evangelism tells a friend about Jesus (word) as she works at the homeless shelter sorting clothing (deed). A man with the gift of healing works as a physician's assistant in a hospital (deed) even as he prays with and comforts a preoperative patient (sign). A gift may demonstrate the ways of Christ in more than one way.

As you study the gifts, you probably will find that you have more than one. A number of gifts may be yours. Often gifts interconnect and complement each other.

Gifts of Word

Apostleship

The gift of apostleship does not mean that you are to become like one of the original twelve apostles. Instead we'll look specifically to the example of Paul, who was also named an apostle. He was a missionary to the church. As a missionary apostle he was **called out by God and sent to a specific people.** He was able to **cross cultural boundaries** to reach people for Jesus Christ and **form new Christian communities.**

Prophecy

This gift does not imply that you should get a nine-hundred number and set up your own psychic hot line or go buy a pack of tarot cards! The word *prophet* means "forth-teller." Think of a prophet as one who can **know past history, see present occurrences, and then understand the bigger picture. A prophet is called to instruct, warn, correct, and forecast the end result.**

Evangelism

Get off your soapbox and put away your bullhorn! Think of people, both introverts and extroverts, shy and outgoing, who **can communicate the gospel message through word and deed.** Are you able to share the good news of Jesus Christ in ways so that people can see, hear, and accept it? Then you may have the gift of evangelism.

Pastoring

This gift is also referred to as shepherding, but don't go buy a herd of sheep. Instead, pull out your **abilities to be a spiritual guide, to sustain people on their journeys, and to work with those who are at different places on the discipleship road.**

Teaching

You don't need a college degree to have the gift of teaching. And just because you are capable of teaching doesn't mean you automatically have the gift. Spiritual teachers have the **ability to clearly explain and effectively apply the truth of Jesus Christ.** Remember, people watch teachers more than others to see if their lifestyles are consistent with their lessons.

Encouragement

The word used in the Bible is *exhortation*, but a more understandable term for us is the word *encouragement*. **Do you come alongside persons to help? Do you work with the lesser able and undergird people to use and do their very best?** This is not a "fix it" person but one who "travels with" another.

Knowledge

Having the gift of knowledge is not being the champion on the popular TV show *Jeopardy* or a winner at Trivial Pursuit. Instead it is **a supernatural ability to stretch beyond the facts and figures to search, make sense of, and bring together the teachings of God for people's lives.**

Wisdom

Wisdom means putting what you know to work in your daily life and helping others to do the same. It is **being in tune with the heart of God** and then living that way. A person with the gift of wisdom weighs all the circumstances in complex situations to find the deeper truth.

Gifts of Deed

Assisting

This gift should carry a warning: "This is not the business of the things we think we *should* do." But if you are one who **assists and lends a helping hand in times of need,** this may be your gift. Do you feel called to give leadership in the distribution of supplies in a disaster area, do the leg work for a group project, or make needed deliveries? Then you may have this gift of assisting and helping others.

Giving

Don't think that if you don't have this gift it means you can ignore the offering plate the next time it's passed! We all are commanded to give. We all have received so much from God that we can't help wanting to give in return. But those with the giving gift **give freely, with a special measure and delight to further God's work in the world.** You also don't have to be rich to have the gift. Remember the Bible story about the widow's mite (Mark 12:41-44)?

Leadership

If you are controlling, domineering, and *need* to be a leader, this gift is not for you! Some Bible translations use the word *government* to name this gift. These gifted individuals are able to **share information and power. They enable those around them to realize and accomplish their goals.** They are good managers and administrators. These persons take leadership roles to equip the church, the Christian community, to work in ways that bring about *God's will*.

Compassion

There are many of us who easily show emotion, but the **ability to empathize with others, stand in their shoes, and then act in ways that help them on their journey** is the essence of the gift of mercy and compassion.

Faith

The Spirit-given **ability to daily see God's will, coupled with the confidence to do it,** is the gift of faith. It is living one day at a time even when life seems out of control. To live fully in faith is to live each day as best you can for who you are in that moment and to trust the rest to God.

Gifts of Sign

Discernment

This is a special ability to **distinguish between truth and error, justice and injustice, what is authentic and genuine and what is phony.** You are able to "see through" people or circumstances to know what is real and what is an illusion, and you have the wisdom and courage to speak or reveal the truth.

Miracles

Are you ready for a miracle? Those with this Spirit-given power are able to **act contrary to natural law or use natural law in extraordinary ways.** This gift is displayed when God's hand miraculously intervenes in your presence in extraordinary ways.

Healing

This is the ability to allow God to work through you as **an instrument for the healing of illness and the restoration of persons' physical, mental, and spiritual health.** (Note of caution: The cure does not depend on the receiving person's faith or the healer's amount of faith.)

Tongues

The sign should read, "NOT FOR CHARISMATICS ONLY." The book of Acts in the New Testament records that on the Day of Pentecost, the tongues spoken were **different languages that normally would not have been spoken** by the people (Acts 2:6). Other times tongues are understood as **verbal utterances that praise God but are not understood by human ears.** Whichever it is, it is a gift to be prized.

Interpretation

Linguistics might be your bag! The gift of interpretation is **the ability to translate when a foreign language is uttered. In a time when we must cross all cultural and language boundaries, this is an invaluable gift.** In the case of ecstatic utterances, as when someone is speaking in tongues, the gift of interpretation can mean to **interpret the nonlinguistic sounds so that the message is understood.**

> Note: The gift of tongues and the gift of interpretation have sometimes been misunderstood. They are legitimate gifts even though in some places and at some times they may not be as commonly evident as some of the other gifts. Keep an open mind as you continue to study these gifts so that you can remain open to the Spirit's work in your own and others' lives.

Some Bible Basics

☞ Display Overhead, page 101.
Participant's Workbook pages 42-43.
You may want to have a different participant each time read the Scripture passage before you share the Bible basic. Instruct the participants to make notes on their worksheets.

1. God Gives Gifts to Everyone.

> Now there are varieties of gifts, but the same Spirit; and there are varieties of services, but the same Lord; and there are varieties of activities, but it is the same God who activates all of them in everyone. To each is given the manifestation of the Spirit for the common good.
>
> 1 CORINTHIANS 12:4-7

This passage from 1 Corinthians says that although our gifts may differ, we all have gifts of the Spirit. Verse 7 states, "To each is given the manifestation of the Spirit"—why?—"for the common good." The text also tells us that "it is the same God who activates all of them in everyone" (verse 6). This "litmus test" helps us determine if the gift comes from the one God. The way we know if the manifestation of the gift is of God is to look at who is served. Does the gift enhance only our own self or does its use extend outward to enhance our Christian community and its mission to the world? Through this service we too grow stronger in our faith. The manifestation of the Spirit promotes spiritual health and builds up the community in faith.

2. God Distributes the Gifts According to God's Grace.

> The gifts he gave were that some would be apostles, some prophets, some evangelists, some pastors and teachers, to equip the saints for the work of ministry, for building up the body of Christ.
>
> EPHESIANS 4:11-12

God gives the gifts as God wills so that we, the saints, can be equipped to do the work of God. The gifts build up and bring unity to the community of Christ. The gifts help us mature to our full potential as persons and as a community. A gift is not something we can demand God to give us. But we can pray when we sense a need and see a vacancy of a particular gift within the community. When we offer a prayer on behalf of the "common good," God's community, it is a selfless prayer. The intent of our prayer is that God will work through us individually or through others to meet the perceived community need.

3. God Promises the Holy Spirit Will Be Our Comforter and Guide.

> "I have said these things to you while I am still with you. But the Advocate, the Holy Spirit, whom the Father will send in my name, will teach you everything, and remind you of all that I have said to you. Peace I leave with you."
>
> JOHN 14:25-27*a*

Jesus promised to send the Holy Spirit, the comforter and guide who would lead the disciples into all truth. The Holy Spirit interprets Christ's teachings and imparts Christ's peace to all believers. These teachings lead us, Christ's followers, to do even greater works.

Some Bible Basics

1. God gives gifts to everyone.

   Read 1 Corinthians 12:4-7.

2. God distributes the gifts according to God's grace.

   Read Ephesians 4:11-12.

3. God promises the Holy Spirit will be our comforter and guide.

   Read John 14:25-27a.

Some Bible Basics

1. God Gives Gifts to Everyone.

> Now there are varieties of gifts, but the same Spirit; and there are varieties of services, but the same Lord; and there are varieties of activities, but it is the same God who activates all of them in everyone. To each is given the manifestation of the Spirit for the common good.
>
> 1 CORINTHIANS 12:4-7

Notes: _____

_____

_____

2. God Distributes the Gifts According to God's Grace.

> The gifts he gave were that some would be apostles, some prophets, some evangelists, some pastors and teachers, to equip the saints for the work of ministry, for building up the body of Christ.
>
> EPHESIANS 4:11-12

Notes: _____

_____

_____

42

3. God Promises the Holy Spirit Will Be Our Comforter and Guide.

> "I have said these things to you while I am still with you. But the Advocate, the Holy Spirit, whom the Father will send in my name, will teach you everything, and remind you of all that I have said to you. Peace I leave with you."
>
> JOHN 14:25-27*a*

Notes: _____

_____

_____

43

Biblical and Contemporary Examples of the Gifts

Apostleship

In the Bible

When we think of apostles, we usually think of the twelve followers called by Jesus during his earthly ministry (see Matthew 10:2). As we read in the Bible, however, the title apostle also was extended to other key leaders in the Christian movement, such as Barnabas and Paul (see Acts 14:14). In Ephesians 3:1-13, Paul claims to be the least of the apostles, commissioned by God's grace. Acts 1:21-26 tells us of another apostle, Matthias, who was chosen to take the place of Judas in ministry. And in Acts 5:12-16, unnamed apostles performed signs and wonders of healing among the people.

In the Bible, persons with the gift of apostleship are missionaries. The Greek word *apostolos* and the Latin word *mission* mean "one who is sent" or "messenger." A missionary is one who lives as Jesus did, as a missional itinerant. Persons with the gift of apostleship are able to minister in a second culture. They give effective leadership in new places for the purpose of teaching the gospel, starting new congregations, and training and enabling leaders. They work to extend God's realm of justice. Second Corinthians 12:12 reminds us that they are persons of outstanding patience. However, as we read in 1 Corinthians 4:8-13, the gift of apostleship is not without cost: apostles are spectacles to the world, fools for the sake of Christ, and are hungry, poorly clothed, and held in disrepute.

Today

Today a person with the gift of apostleship might be called a pioneer missionary. Roben is such a missionary who serves in the inner city. Living in a parsonage next door to her congregation, she sees the hard street life of drugs and violence. Yet Roben, who is a single parent of two young children, feels called to minister there. Roben, an Anglo, reaches out in the name of Christ to her Spanish-speaking neighborhood. By playing midnight basketball with African American and Hispanic males, she establishes God's presence. She shares Christ's love through contemporary worship with the gay and lesbian community. She is in ministry with the people. Roben is truly a person with the gift of apostleship.

Prophecy

In the Bible

Persons who receive and communicate a message from God have the gift of prophecy. They have a special ability to listen to God. Prophets see and speak the will of God for a specific people, time, and place. In the book of Acts we find several examples of the gift of prophecy. In Acts 11:27-28, Agabus, a follower of Christ, predicts there will be a severe famine throughout the region—a prediction that later comes true. In Acts 20:10, Paul bends over a gravely ill man and rightly announces that the man will live. Acts 21:9 tells us that Philip, the evangelist, had four daughters, all with the gift of prophecy.

The book of Acts also portrays the disciple Peter's use of the gift of prophecy. In chapters 1 and 2, Peter repeatedly uses the Hebrew Scripture to validate his spoken truths. Later, in chapter 5, he is able to identify evil motives of Ananias and Sapphira, who lied to the congregation about what they had given.

We see that Peter is bold and forthright with others concerning God's demands on their lives, directing them to align their lives with God and leading them to repentance and baptism.

Like Peter, persons with the gift of prophecy possess a burning desire to serve by proclaiming God's truth. Prophets have a strong sense of duty, yet they must remember to temper their gift of prophecy with love so that they do more good than harm.

Today

When we think of the prophetic voices of this century, Dr. Martin Luther King Jr. comes to mind. Dr. King was a man of God who had a dream. He spoke out on freedom, nonviolence, and civil rights in a thoughtful, intelligent, and provocative manner. He was determined to achieve justice and equality for all people. His message is as relevant today as it was during his lifetime. Persons throughout the world continue to be inspired by his vision, passion, and faith. Through his commitment, courage, and dedication, he is esteemed as a prophet for our time.

Evangelism

In the Bible

The gift of evangelism enables persons to reach beyond their usual sphere of influence to share the gospel and God's love. Peter, by word and example, does so in Acts 2:14-21. Evangelists are able to help others see their lives clearly in the context of God's grace, moving them to life-changing decisions. They realize they cannot take credit for a person coming to faith because it is God's doing, as we read in 1 Corinthians 3:5-9. Through the ministry of evangelists, seekers come to know the truth (see 1 Timothy 2:1-7), place their faith in God, and become Jesus' disciples. Yet the gift of evangelism does not end there. People with this gift go on to help persons become grounded and formed as Christian disciples.

In Acts 8:4-8, the disciple Philip demonstrates the gift of evangelism while in Samaria. The people accept Christ as they are "hearing and seeing the signs that he did." Philip witnesses as he proclaims the good news and cures the lame. In another story, found in Acts 8:26-40, Philip evangelizes a man from Ethiopia who works for the queen. Together they study the Scriptures. The Ethiopian asks Philip, "What is to prevent me from being baptized?" Philip baptizes the man who has accepted Christ as the new ruler of his life.

Today

Leon is a man with a mission, a mission that began with a yearning to reach out to men in prison. Today he has engineered the first Kairos prison ministry* in his state. Through a three-day in-house spiritual retreat, these incarcerated men hear, many for the first time, about the love of Christ and their own worthiness. They come to understand that Christ came to earth especially so that they might live. Leon also is the leader of an out-prison ministry that assists released prisoners to get on their feet. He not only has the ability to organize, but he also is able to share a vision that catches other people's attention and energy. Leon demonstrates his passionate love of people as he shares the greatest gift of all: Jesus.

---

*An adaptation of the Roman Catholic Cursillo, Episcopalian Cursillo, Tres Dias, and the Walk of Emmaus, Kairos prison ministry is an ecumenical project in which volunteers minister with incarcerated persons.

Pastoring

In the Bible

As we read in 1 Timothy 3:1-7, those with the gift of pastoring are able to counsel and encourage followers. They are able to mentor others in their discipleship journeys because they have already traveled the road. They take responsibility to care for a group of believers over the long haul. Like the follower Titus, they use Scripture reading and teaching to reinforce their preaching (see Titus 1:9). They call persons to accountable discipleship and intercede when someone wanders away from holy living. They keep a watchful eye for the well-being of others. These spiritual, people-centered persons patiently pray for others, desiring them to grow spiritually as disciples.

In Jesus we see the heart of a pastor. John 14 illustrates Jesus' pastoring characteristics. In verse 9, Jesus shows the disciples the error of their way. In verses 11-14, he patiently shares truth with them as he senses they are able to hear and accept it. Then he teaches them of the Holy Spirit in verses 16 and 17. Throughout the Gospels we see that Jesus cares for the spiritual well-being of his primary disciples, as well as for many other friends in ministry, including Mary and Martha. Jesus is the Great Shepherd.

Today

Diedra has been a seminary professor for many years. Her office and home are welcome places for students and faculty. She demonstrates tough love as she shares unqualified acceptance with those who come to her door. As a teacher of the Word, she draws on the Holy Scriptures to call persons to accountability. Diedra is a woman in touch with her own spirituality. She asks frequently, through her words and actions, if all is "well with your soul." She cares deeply for all those entrusted to her care.

Teaching

In the Bible

Persons with the gift of teaching have the ability to bring new believers into maturity. They live God's will through personal study and teaching others. They communicate in a manner that brings persons to understand and apply the learnings. This leads to informed, healthy ministry within the congregation. They teach disciples how to live in just ways. Persons with the gift of teaching also teach other teachers, so that even more persons may learn. In this way the Word is passed from person to person and generation to generation.

Acts 2:42 shows that teaching was a foundational act of the early church. Barnabas was a teacher in both Antioch and Tarsus. As we read in Acts 11:24, "he was a good man, full of the Holy Spirit and of faith." Through his gift he brought Christ to a great many people. He and Paul spent an entire year with one congregation in Antioch. It was there that the disciples were first called Christians.

Today

Patricia leads spiritual formation workshops and seminars. She is frequently asked, "What are your gifts?" The one gift she names without hesitation is teaching. She finds as much joy in preparation as she does in presentation.

Acknowledging her gift as a wonderful opportunity and a tremendous responsibility, she works hard to prepare her lessons. She uses the best methodologies so that those in her care will be able to gain spiritual content and wisdom. Patricia always recalls James's warning: "Not many of you should become teachers, my brothers and sisters, for you know that we who teach will be judged with greater strictness" (James 3:1). Therefore she always seeks divine guidance. The true test of a teacher is her or his life.

Encouragement

In the Bible

Comfort, consolation, and counsel are three primary roles of the gift of encouragement. Persons with this gift care for others in ways that empower them to be helped and healed. Encouragement is modeled in 1 Thessalonians 2:11 as a parental role. The apostle Paul writes, "We dealt with each one of you like a father with his children, urging and encouraging you and pleading that you lead a life worthy of God." As we read in Acts 14:22, encouragement was esteemed as most important to the community in times of persecution.

Timothy, an early church leader, had the gift of encouragement. We read in 2 Timothy 1:5 how his grandmother, Eunice, and mother, Lois—both women with the gift of encouragement—had first nurtured him as a child. In his First Letter to Timothy, the apostle Paul refers to Timothy's gift of encouragement as well as demonstrates his own use of the gift of encouragement: "Until I arrive, give attention to the public reading of scripture, to exhorting, to teaching. Do not neglect the gift that is in you" (4:13-14*a*). Paul's enduring relationship with Timothy encouraged and strengthened him during difficult times. Because of his gift of encouragement, Timothy was Paul's closest companion.

Today

Jeanette, a woman in full-time ministry, is filled with the gift of encouragement. She oversees the daily work of pastors entrusted to her care. She travels from congregation to congregation and house to house giving words of inspiration and comfort. She motivates those who need a bit of a push and comforts others who need reassurance. She exemplifies the charge in 1 Thessalonians 5:14 to "admonish the idlers, encourage the faint hearted, help the weak, be patient with all of them." Through a visit, letter, or phone call, she follows the Romans 12:15 instruction to "rejoice with those who rejoice, weep with those who weep."

Knowledge

In the Bible

As we read in Colossians 2:2, persons with the gift of knowledge are able to perceive and understand the mystery of God's will and ways. They have an earnest hunger to know divine, timeless truths. These truths are linked to the call for justice and righteousness. Knowledge is important for the health and well-being of the Body of Christ. In 1 Corinthians 12 we see that wisdom and knowledge are closely related. Paul prays in Colossians 1:9 that "you may be filled with the knowledge of God's will in all spiritual wisdom and understanding." Through his own gift of knowledge, Paul is able to acquire deep insight into divine truth.

Today

David is a person who searches, systematizes, and summarizes the teachings of God. His ability is closely related to the gift of teaching. In fact, he is an excellent teacher. David does not have knowledge at the expense of common sense. Instead, his knowledge directs his experience. David equips others for the work of ministry by sharing his gift of knowledge so that they can "grow in the grace and knowledge of our Lord and Savior Jesus Christ" (2 Peter 3:18). Through his efforts, numerous young people have entered full-time ministry.

Wisdom

In the Bible

When God reveals insight or direction about a particular problem to a person, that person has the gift of wisdom. Persons with this gift link their understandings of life with keen insights into the ways of God. In this way they know what to do and how to do it. First Corinthians 1:25 and 3:18-19 remind those with the gift of wisdom that God's wisdom is stronger than human wisdom. In Acts 6:3-4, seven men are selected, "full of the Spirit and of wisdom," to care for the needs of the whole community. Persons with the gift of wisdom are able to use information at the right time, in the right way. They reason and solve problems according to God's will.

Today

Dale is a man of wisdom. He uses his gift of insight and accumulated knowledge as he advocates world peace. Dale understands how knowledge and experience can be applied to specific needs of the world. He is able to grasp and order the deep truths of God's world. As he meets with governmental policy makers, he relates these truths to the needs and problems of life. Speaking on behalf of world peace before large audiences, he has the ability to apply his wisdom to complex situations. He weighs the true nature of the situation and then exercises spiritual insight into its rightness or wrongness. Dale uses his gift of wisdom as a maker of peace.

Assisting

In the Bible

Persons with the gift of assisting have the ability to bring support to those in need. In 1 Timothy 3:8, assisters called "deacons" are called to be "serious, not double-tongued, not indulging in much wine, not greedy for money; they must hold fast to the mystery of the faith with a clear conscience." Phoebe, a deacon named in Romans 16:1-2, demonstrates this special gift by giving aid to others so that they can increase the effective use of their own gifts. In 2 Timothy 1:16, Paul grants a special blessing upon the household of Onesiphorus because of his work of enablement.

Assisters sense a need and give support for the greater good of the community. In the book of Philippians, Epaphroditus offers his gift of assisting with a spirit of eagerness and joy. The text tells us how he "came close to death for the work of Christ." As Epaphroditus recognized, sometimes the gift can even demand that one lay down her or his life for another.

Today

Sally and Simon, now in their eighties, have lived a lifetime helping others. Sally is always ready to cut out the hand work for a busy Sunday school teacher, prepare a church mailing, deliver flowers, or prepare the Lord's Supper. Simon, also a ready aid, has served as a trustee for many years. Always close at hand, he helps neighbors in need, delivers meals to the elderly, ushers at the Sunday service, paints the fellowship hall, hangs a window, or stops a leaky faucet. Simon's and Sally's work frees others to serve more effectively. Their congregation and community are blessed by their gift.

Giving

In the Bible

Persons with the gift of giving have the special ability to give cheerfully and liberally to support the ongoing work of God. They are able to harness and manage monetary resources in ways that give power to further God's business. They give with simplicity, as described in Romans 12:8. Their joy and eagerness are unsurpassed as they follow the command of Christ in Matthew 6:3: "Do not let your left hand know what your right hand is doing." Barnabas is singled out for special mention in the book of Acts. In 4:34-37 we read how he sells land and brings the money to the apostles. Persons with the gift of giving benefit others and aid the work of God's reign in the world.

Today

Glenn and Bette are esteemed models of the gift of giving. Whether it's handing out food, collecting blankets for the homeless, or buying ice cream for the neighborhood children, they give such care and cheer that the recipients are fortified. It is not that they have many possessions. Rather, they share what they do have with any who are in need. These two believers are special stewards. They have discovered this Spirit-bestowed gift and derive genuine joy from seeing God work through their gift. They delight in using temporal possessions for God's glory and their neighbors' good.

Leadership

In the Bible

Persons with this gift are able to lead others effectively. In 1 Timothy 3:5, the apostle Paul gives Timothy some common sense related to recruiting leaders: "For if someone does not know how to manage his own household, how can he take care of God's church?"

God-empowered leaders have the ability to elicit trust. Persons with the gift share the vision of God's *shalom* in ways that capture the imagination. They use their leadership energies and skills for the good of the community. They set goals and communicate the desired results to others. They do all of these things so that God's will is accomplished.

Leaders care for the spiritual well-being of persons entrusted to their care. Hebrews 13:17 says that leaders "are keeping watch over your souls and will give an account. Let them do this with joy and not with sighing." Those with the gift create "safe space" for others to function and use their unique spiritual gifts.

Today

Susan is a woman of conviction who has the gift of leadership. In her work, her congregation, or her immediate family, Susan helps groups work harmoniously to accomplish their goals. Plans run smoothly as she thoughtfully considers the pros and cons of decisions, big and little. This gifted woman is able to mobilize people to accomplish God's mission and ministry. She can claim the New Testament compliment found in 1 Timothy 5:17: "Let the elders who rule well be considered worthy of double honor, especially those who labor in preaching and teaching."

Compassion

In the Bible

Tabitha was a disciple who had the gift of compassion. We learn in Acts 9:36 that throughout her hometown of Joppa she "was devoted to good works and acts of charity." The gift of compassion enabled her to have genuine empathy for others, both Christians and non-Christians. She joyfully translated her compassion into good works. Her deeds of kindness reflect God's love.

Like Tabitha, persons with the gift of compassion have a special ability to work with the afflicted, poor, and abused. They care for the "least of these," as Jesus taught his followers in Matthew 25:42-45.

Today

Mother Teresa is known by many for her gift of compassion. For years she has worked with the poorest of India. In addition to her continuing work in Calcutta, she travels the globe as a spokesperson for the outcast and downtrodden of the world. We often see pictures of her sincerely smiling into the camera or bending lovingly over a person in need. She does not work grudgingly or out of a sense of duty alone. She is a constant source of inspiration to all and an exceptional example of a person with the gift of compassion.

Faith

In the Bible

The entire chapter of Hebrews 11 describes the gift of faith in detail: "Now faith is the assurance of things hoped for, the conviction of things not seen" (v. 1). Persons with the gift of faith have extraordinary confidence in God's faithfulness. Because of their gift, they help the faith community find assurance as they do the work of ministry. Jesus teaches about faith in Matthew 17:20: "For truly I tell you, if you have faith the size of a mustard seed, you will say to this mountain, 'Move from here to there,' and it will move; and nothing will be impossible for you." Persons with this gift may not desire to move physical mountains, but through their gift they enable the church to "keep on keeping on" in faithfulness to God's calling.

Today

Ada would be the last to boast of having the gift of faith. Instead, she sees herself as a woman who has done the best she can through the years and left the rest in God's hands. She prays that God will find her worthy when the trumpet sounds for her to return home. In her eighty-plus years, Ada has raised seven children and buried a coal mining husband who died of black lung. Through the lean times, she has cared for herself and her family. In faith to Christ, she has given generous aid to her home congregation, helped to establish the local fire department, and cared for other community needs. When her home and small country store serving a backwoods community burned down, she picked through the rubble and began again. Her community respects her, and her children and grandchildren call her blessed. Ada is a woman of faith.

Discernment

In the Bible

Persons with the gift of discernment are able to look beyond certain behaviors and circumstances to determine if they are good or evil, right or wrong. They call persons to accountability, as Jesus does in Matthew 7:5: "You hypocrite, first take the log out of your own eye, and then you will see clearly to take the speck out of your neighbor's eye." They look through apparent issues and see underlying truths. They make judgments concerning what is and what is not of God. In Acts 5:1-6, the apostle Peter brings to accountability two persons who have lied to the community.

Persons with the gift of discernment bring health and wholeness to the community of Christ. Because they are able to analyze what inclinations should be encouraged and what tendencies should be discouraged in brothers and sisters of the faith, they are valuable in personal counseling situations. In 1 John 4:1 we read, "Beloved, do not believe every spirit, but test the spirits to see whether they are from God." Some persons with the gift are able to perform this task better than others.

Today

Al is a person with the gift of discernment. Because of his keen insights, leaders appreciate having Al attend their meetings. He calls group dynamics into question and asks persons to be accountable for their actions. Al "sees through" persons to the spiritual needs within. He picks up subtle hints that tell him when people are at odds with what they are saying. Having the ability to see through the facade, he differentiates between what is raised up by God and what pretends to be. He has the uncanny ability to unmask false teachings and ways. Al is valuable in helping others pinpoint and assess their gifts to find their niche in the mission and ministry of the community. Al is an excellent spiritual mentor and guide.

Miracles

In the Bible

Three words are used in the Bible in connection with miracles: power, wonder, and sign. Acts 5:12 states: "Now many signs and wonders were done among the people through the apostles." In the most restrictive interpretation, persons with the gift of miracles participate with God to do powerful works that transcend and alter the ordinary course of nature as we know it. These supernatural works demonstrate God's love and power. In Acts 5:15-16, Peter casts a shadow that heals many. Observers perceive that the ordinary course of fate has been altered. After Tabitha, a godly woman, dies, Peter raises her from the dead. Likewise, in Acts 20:7-12, Paul revives Eutychus, a young man who has fallen to his death. True miracles, like these, are palpable to the senses. Acts 8:6-8 reports the sign miracles that the disciple Philip accorded. Miracles are evidence in order to authenticate the divine commission to bring in the reign and realm of God. In a broader sense, miracles are an unusual and timely providential interference in human affairs. Persons with this gift witness remarkable answers to prayer, extra strength in times of need, abundant provision in scarcity, and timely protection in danger. These human intermediaries are able to help free others from what prevents them from fulfilling their ministry. These blockages are related to the body, mind, and spirit.

111

Today

Pamela has witnessed miracles in her presence many times. She acknowledges that God does not usually choose miracles to intervene in our lives, yet, as a hospital chaplain at a major medical center, she does not deny the evidence of their occurrences. She never tries to explain away a miracle. Instead, she accepts miracles for what they are: signs of God's continuous presence and activity in the world.

Pamela reminds us that Jesus' calming the sea was important, but not any more remarkable than calming the anxious hearts of loved ones as they sit at the deathbed of their beloved mother. Feeding the four thousand was grand, but how beneficial it is for the hungry children of Rwanda finally to receive long awaited food supplies. Raising the dead is amazing, but how marvelous it is to witness a person, once dying from drugs and alcohol, receive eternal life. Jesus promised his followers would "do greater works than these" (John 14:12). This promise is being fulfilled today. Those deaf to God hear the Word. The lame begin to walk in righteousness. The selfish find new purpose, and those who do wrong make restitution.

Healing

In the Bible

Numerous examples of healing power, worked through Jesus Christ during his ministry on earth, are recorded in Scripture. A paralyzed man is lowered down to Jesus through a roof and later walks out (Luke 5:17-26), a rich man's servant is cured (Matthew 8:5-13), and one with a withered hand is revived with a touch (Mark 3:1-6)—all testifying to Jesus' abilities. Matthew 9:35 states: "Jesus went about all the cities and villages . . . curing every disease and every sickness."

The gift of healing continued in the works of the disciples after Jesus' death. Peter healed a lame man (Acts 3:6-8), Stephen did great signs and wonders of healing (Acts 6:8), Philip cured those of unclean spirits (Acts 8:5-8), Paul healed a crippled person in Lystra (Acts 14:8-10), and many healing miracles occurred in the city of Ephesus (Acts 19:11-12). Persons with the gift of healing have the ability to cure or be cured of ill conditions that hinder effective ministries for Christ, the church, or other persons.

Today

David, a layperson, felt led to begin a healing ministry and worship service in his church. David takes seriously the instructions in James 5:14-16: "Are any among you sick? They should call for the elders of the church and have them pray over them, anointing them with oil in the name of the Lord" (v. 14).

Through his ministry, David has witnessed many healings. He realizes that healings happen through those who are open to God working in their lives. He is willing to serve as a human intermediary for the healing of himself and others. Many have come to David, either through worship services or in one-on-one visits. They have been cured of illness and restored to health. They are witnesses to God's healing power which brings wholeness to one's mind, body, and spirit.

Other persons within David's congregation also have named and claimed healing as their gift. Although David was the first to acknowledge God's work through his life, evidenced by healing, now others join him in this ministry. A counseling center has been opened in the church. A spiritual network is in place, helping persons learn disciplined spiritual formation. An Alcoholics Anonymous group recently started meeting in the church's education building. Spiritual and physical health are being restored, not only in the immediate congregation but also within the broader community.

Tongues

In the Bible

The biblical gift of tongues is manifested in two ways. In Acts 2:1-13 it seems to refer to a foreign language. On the day of Pentecost, the disciples spoke in dialects that were not their native tongues. They received a message from God and, through a divinely anointed utterance, communicated it with others in languages the disciples themselves had never learned. This occurred so that people from many nations could hear the message of Christ.

A second use of the gift of tongues appears in 1 Corinthians 12–14. Here we see persons with the ability to speak in an unknown language for private devotion and edification. Speaking in tongues, according to these descriptions, is not a naturally learned ability. Persons speak to God in an unknown language, one they could never have learned. Their speech sometimes is referred to as "ecstatic utterances."

For the early church, tongues offered evidence of the new reality of Christ's kingdom. In 1 Corinthians 14:22, tongues "are a sign not for believers but for unbelievers." This is why the gift of tongues is designated as a sign gift. First Corinthians 14:2 tells us that tongues speak to God and speak of the mysteries of the Spirit. As with all the gifts, tongues primarily serve to build the Christian community, the Body of Christ.

Today

Although their experiences differ, both Bill and Jim have the gift of tongues. Bill learns new second languages with ease. He is not sure why this is so. He speaks five languages. He teaches at a major university and suffers along with students who struggle to learn even the most basic structure of a new language. Bill hears a person speaking a dialect and is able to decipher enough of what the person is saying to communicate with her or him. He claims this as a gift from God, for surely he has not done anything under his own power to have this ability. Bill uses his gift in ministry with his inner-city congregation where numerous cultures and languages coexist.

Jim possesses what is referred to as "ecstatic utterances." These verbal manifestations do not correspond with any known language. He is careful in the use of his gift, because he does not want to construct linguistic barriers within the community. Instead, his gift reassures and strengthens him and others even as it praises and glorifies God. His God-given gift for speaking in tongues offers the congregation evidence that God is doing a new thing in the midst of them. His gift is understood as a sign from God, edifying the church. Jim's pastor and worshiping community accept his gift as being of God, for they see the Spirit's work in Jim as he grows in grace and as his life bears the fruit of the Spirit.

Interpretation

In the Bible

The gift of interpretation is manifested in two ways in the Bible. First, it is the special ability God gives individuals to make known what is being communicated by the person who speaks in tongues or "ecstatic utterances." In 1 Corinthians 12:10, the interpretation of tongues is listed immediately after the gift of tongues. This is for good reason. According to 1 Corinthians 14, the early church encountered a problem related to interpretation. In 1 Corinthians 14:13 and 26, Paul suggests that someone should interpret when unknown tongues are spoken so that confusion does not occur. The person with the gift of interpretation uses common speech to convey to others the message of the one who speaks in tongues—all this so that the Body of Christ, the congregation of God's people, can be uplifted.

The second use of the gift of interpretation is the ability to interpret language and meanings of words. Persons with the gift of interpretation may be linguists, who are accomplished in languages and speech forms and may utilize their gift vocationally. Specifically, they use their gift to reveal a spiritual message, thereby enhancing the growth of persons within the community. As recorded in Acts 8:26-40, the disciple Philip joined the Ethiopian in his chariot to interpret his readings. Philip served as God's instrument to lead the man to Christ.

Today

Both Philip and Mary have the gift of interpretation, although the way they express the gift differs. Philip serves in ministry with an international Bible translation group. He speaks a number of languages fluently and deciphers dialects with little trouble. As a linguist, his lifework is to study human speech—its units, nature, structure, and modifications. Philip helps to make translations of the Scriptures available in various languages around the globe. He also has helped to write a translator's handbook on one of the Gospels, which aids translators in working to convey the total message of the gospel.

Mary's gift enables her to convey to others, in a language they understand, what is being uttered by the one who speaks in tongues. When the congregation assembles, her gift is called upon when someone speaks in tongues, as in "ecstatic utterances." Mary uses her gift to discern the message of the speaker. Sometimes Mary also speaks in tongues, interpreting her own utterances for those gathered. Mary knows her gift is an important one in the congregation. In fact, unless her gift of interpretation is present, the person with the gift of tongues may be unable to exercise his or her gift. Mary takes seriously Paul's advice in 1 Corinthians 14:13 and 26. She wants to help prevent the confusion experienced by the early church.

Gift Versus Roles and Works of Ministry

👉 *Participant's Workbook* page 63.

A gift is not necessarily the same as a role or work of ministry, although gifts are lived out in the roles we take and the works of ministry in which we participate. Roles and works are the vehicles through which our gifts are lived daily in tangible ways. A gift is a specific calling upon our lives. How we live out that calling is seen in the roles and works we undertake. Gifts, unlike roles and works, cannot be earned or learned.

You may not have the gift of giving, but as a member of Christ's church, you are called to give when the offering plate is passed and to follow the example of the widow who gave even her last pennies (Mark 12:42). You may not have the gift of evangelism, but you are commanded to witness for Jesus Christ (Matthew 28:19-20). So what's the difference?

A person with the gift places a high priority on the gift in his or her life. A person with the gift of giving may spend much time and energy raising money and distributing it to the glory of God. Those of us without the gift simply incorporate giving into our lives as one of the many ways we serve God and live out our Christian discipleship. A person with the gift of evangelism has a passion to share the gospel and may give much creative energy to evangelizing efforts and strategies. The rest of us simply share the gospel with those we come into contact with in our everyday lives.

👉 Allow time for questions before having the participants complete their worksheets.

Gifts Versus Roles and Works of Ministry

A gift is not necessarily the same as a role or work of ministry. A gift is a specific calling upon own lives. How we live out that calling is seen in the roles and works we undertake.

You may not have the gift of giving, but as a member of Christ's church, you are called to give when the offering plate is passed and to follow the example of the widow who gave even her last pennies (Mark 12:42). You may not have the gift of evangelism, but you are commanded to witness for Jesus Christ (Matthew 28:19-20). So what's the difference?

A person with the gift places a high priority on the gift in his or her life. A person with the gift of giving may spend much time and energy raising money and distributing it to the glory of God. Those of us without the gift simply incorporate giving into our lives as one of the many ways we serve God and live out our Christian discipleship.

List below the roles and works of ministry that are high priorities in your life.

Do any of these coincide with the gifts you have identified in your life? Circle these.

Do any cause you to wonder if you may have unrecognized gifts? Underline these.

63

LEADER

Gifts Versus Talents and Abilities

☞ *Participant's Workbook* pages 64-65.

A gift is not a natural or acquired talent or ability. We all have talents and abilities and skills that we have acquired through practice or that seem to be innate. Gifts, on the other hand, can only be given to us by God.

Ms. Frye is a Sunday school teacher who makes the hour seem long and the lessons boring. Mr. Blank, on the other hand, is a teacher who gives students a passion for learning the Scriptures and excitement in their labor. It is one thing to learn the skills and proper techniques of teaching. It is an entirely different matter to possess the gift of teaching that inspires students. Ms. Frye may have acquired teaching skills, but Mr. Blank possesses the gift of teaching.

Mrs. Smith, a piano teacher, can tell you which of her students have learned the skills of playing and can get through the scales with precision. She also can enthusiastically tell you about those whose passion for music touches the very soul. Such a person's piano playing may be her or his way of using the gift of evangelism to share the gospel of Jesus Christ, or it may be her or his way of living out a specific gift, such as sharing compassion with persons in need of God's sustaining presence. In other words, individuals use talents and abilities as expressions of God-given gifts.

Some persons appear to have a gift in the form of a talent or ability, but they are not followers of Jesus Christ. What about these persons? We believe that the Holy Spirit is at work before, during, and after a person's baptism. Even our ability to be obedient to Christ is not our work; it is God's work. We cannot take credit. By the same token, the Holy Spirit, God's Spirit, is always at work in each individual, functioning to bring that person to the full knowledge of God's love through Jesus Christ. Each person we meet is of sacred worth. We need to remember that God is already at work in the people we encounter.

☞ Allow time for questions and discussion before having the participants complete their worksheets.

Gifts Versus Talents and Abilities

A gift is not a natural or acquired talent or ability. We all have talents and abilities and skills that we have acquired through practice or that seem to be innate. Gifts, on the other hand, can only be given to us by God.

Ms. Frye is a Sunday school teacher who makes the hour seem long and the lessons boring. Mr. Blank, on the other hand, is a teacher who gives students a passion for learning the Scriptures and excitement in their labor. It is one thing to learn the skills and proper techniques of teaching. It is an entirely different matter to possess the gift of teaching that inspires students. Ms. Frye may have acquired teaching skills, but Mr. Blank possesses the gift of teaching.

Mrs. Smith, a piano teacher, can tell you which of her students have learned the skills of playing and can get through the scales with precision. She also can enthusiastically tell you about those whose passion for music touches the very soul. Such a person's piano playing may be her or his way of using the gift of evangelism to share the gospel of Jesus Christ, or it may be her or his way of living out a specific gift, such as sharing compassion, with persons in need of God's sustaining presence. In other words, individuals use talents and abilities as expressions of God-given gifts.

Some persons appear to have a gift in the form of a talent or ability, but they are not followers of Jesus Christ. What about these persons? We believe that the Holy Spirit is at work before, during, and after a person's baptism. Even our ability to be obedient to Christ is not our work; it is God's work. We cannot take credit. The Holy Spirit, God's Spirit, is always at work in each individual, functioning to bring that person to the full knowledge of God's love through Jesus Christ. Each person we meet is of sacred worth. We need to remember that God is already at work in the people we encounter.

On the next page, list your natural or acquired talents and abilities.

64

How do you use these as expressions of gifts of the Spirit? Write the corresponding gift or gifts beside each talent or ability listed above.

65

LEADER

What Will the Gift Look Like When I See It?

☞ *Participant's Workbook* page 66.

Now that we have reviewed descriptions of the gifts of the Spirit and have discussed how gifts differ from roles, works, talents, and abilities, let's consider in greater depth some of the specific gifts we have identified in ourselves and the roles, works, talents, or abilities that might emerge from them.

This is a two-way exercise that will help you *own* gifts that you have identified by revealing *evidences* of your gifts seen in roles, works, talents, or abilities. As you see and hear the examples of others, you also will recognize ways you may use your gifts.

☞ Ask the participants to work in pairs for approximately ten minutes, completing the exercise first for one and then the other. The first person to take a turn names his or her top three gifts. Then, for each gift, the pair brainstorm actual or possible evidences of the gift in the person's life. Present and discuss the overhead *What Will the Gift Look Like When I See It?* as an example before the group begins.

What Will the Gift Look Like When I See It?

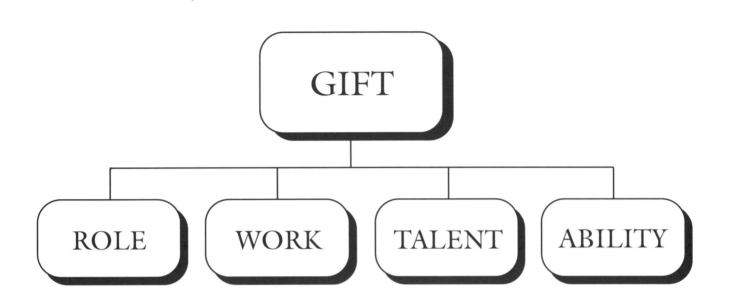

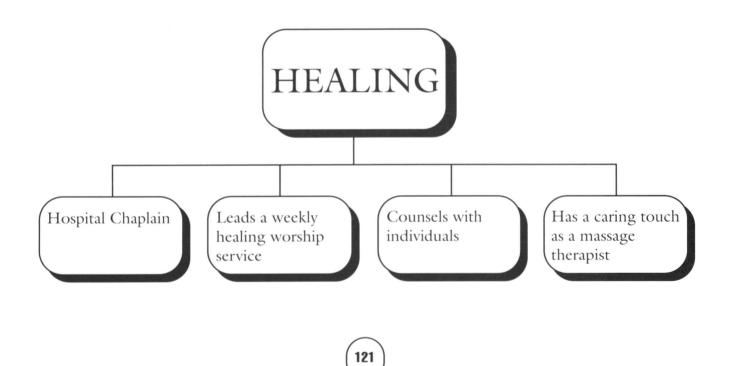

What Will the Gift Look Like When I See It?

Reread the descriptions of your top three gifts of the Spirit as identified by the spiritual gifts survey (pages 31-35). Then list the roles, works, talents, and abilities that you see or would like to see emerging from these gifts.

EXAMPLE:

Gift of the Spirit	*Roles, Works, Talents, Abilities*
Healing	hospital chaplain; leading healing worship service; drug counseling; massage therapist; hospital visitor; supportive listening

Gift of the Spirit	*Roles, Works, Talents, Abilities*
1.	
2.	
3.	

66

Patterns of My Life

☞ *Participant's Workbook* page 67.

Life events and activities can give us clues about our spiritual gifts. This exercise will help you identify those events and activities that, when viewed with a broader lens, reveal repeating patterns. Sometimes we are too close to our own lives to see these patterns and recognize their significance. By working with a partner, who will serve as your "listener," you will begin to see and understand the patterns of your own life.

Jan and John are examples of persons who have taken such an inventory of their lives. On the *Patterns of My Life* worksheet, Jan listed her successful fund drive for the community library five years ago. She also included her involvement in developing the new stewardship materials for her congregation, as well as her work with Habitat for Humanity. Last year she was instrumental in getting donations for all the materials and labor necessary to construct a new home. Together Jan and her listener saw a pattern emerge involving the raising and distributing of funds. This proved to be valuable information as she continued to review the material about spiritual gifts, particularly the gift of giving.

On his worksheet, John listed his employment as a clinical psychologist, a vocation he finds both challenging and rewarding. John also included his involvement with the local volunteer fire company, where he serves as chaplain. Finally, John noted that he utilizes his Red Cross training in first aid by volunteering his time after worship services on Sundays to take persons' blood pressure. After seeing a common thread, John's listener suggested that John study the gifts of compassion and healing to see if one of these might be his gift.

☞ Instruct the participants to complete part A of the worksheet. When everyone is finished, have the group break into pairs and complete part B. Each pair should designate one person the "talker" and the other the "listener." Tell them that they have twenty minutes to complete the exercise. When half the time is up, have them reverse roles.

Patterns of My Life

A. List five life events or activities in which you have done something that you have found rewarding or fulfilling. These might be things you do fairly well.

1. _____

2. _____

3. _____

4. _____

5. _____

B. Find a partner. Designate one of you "talker" and the other "listener." Then spend approximately ten minutes focusing on the life events or activities listed by the talker. The talker's role is to describe the events or activities he or she has listed, sharing personal stories as appropriate. The listener's role is to use who, what, when, where, and why questions to find clarity and concrete evidence of any repeating patterns. After ten minutes, reverse roles and repeat the exercise. Note any findings below:

67

LEADER

Discerning Our Gifts in Community

☞ *Participant's Workbook* page 68.

Print the names of each spiritual gift on a 4" x 11" or larger piece of paper. Be sure the signs are readable from across the room. Hang each sign on the wall, placing them side by side, four to six feet apart.

Throughout the SpiritGifts program we have been discerning our gifts in the context of community as we have shared in discussions and activities together. Now we will be even more intentional in looking to one another for help in discerning our gifts by sharing with others the gifts we think are ours. At the same time, we will help another person examine her or his gifts.

☞ A. If you are leading a group of twenty persons or more, read the following instructions. If your group has fewer than twenty persons, read the instructions under B., below.

The signs posted around the room name the gifts of the Spirit. Each of you is to stand under the sign that names what you think is your number one gift. Write the names of the others who join you there on your worksheet. When I indicate time is up, move to your number two gift and write down the names of the persons you find there. Again, when I indicate time is up, proceed to your number three gift and write down the names of the persons standing with you. Remember not to move until I give the word. We will wait until everyone has had the opportunity to write down all the names in the group.

Now, proceed to your number one gift.

☞ Allow time for the activity.

Now I invite you to choose someone from your lists who has one of the same gifts as you. Sit down with this person and discuss the following questions:
1. Why do you think you have this gift?
2. How do you live out this gift in concrete actions?
3. What do the two of you have in common related to how you live out this gift?

☞ B. If you are leading a group of fewer than twenty persons, read the following instructions.

As I stand under each of the spiritual gifts signs, I will invite you to come stand with me if that gift is one of your top three gifts. When you arrive, write on your worksheet the names of the others standing with you. We will do this for all eighteen gifts.

☞ Allow time for the activity.

Now find one other person who has one of the same gifts as you and sit down with this person to discuss the following questions:
1. Why do you think you have this gift?
2. How do you live out this gift in concrete actions?
3. What do the two of you have in common related to how you live out this gift?

Discerning Our Gifts in Community

Write what you believe are your top three gifts on the lines below. Then listen for further instructions.

1. Gift: _____
Names:

2. Gift: _____
Names:

3. Gift: _____
Names:

Now sit down with one of the persons on your list and discuss why each of you thinks you have this gift. How do each of you live out the gift in concrete action? What do you have in common? What are your differences? Write what you learn from your discussion. If possible, repeat this exercise for each gift.

NOTES:

68

Responsive Listening Bible Study

1 C O R I N T H I A N S 1 2 : 1 2 - 2 6

☞ *Participant's Workbook* pages 69-70.

These verses from 1 Corinthians 12 are central to the SpiritGifts program. They communicate that the goal of the Spirit's work is the building of the community. It is important that participants become familiar and interact with these verses through the use of Responsive Listening Bible Study. Have the participants break into small groups and follow the step-by-step instructions for Responsive Listening Bible Study (*Participant's Workbook* pages 19-20, *Leader's Resources* pages 61-62).

During the study, walk from group to group, asking what step the group is on and if they have any questions or concerns. Be attuned to groups who get bogged down and to facilitators who do not keep their groups moving through the steps as described.

For just as the body is one and has many members, and all the members of the body, though many, are one body, so it is with Christ. For in the one Spirit we were all baptized into one body—Jews or Greeks, slaves or free—and we were all made to drink of one Spirit.

Indeed, the body does not consist of one member but of many. If the foot would say, "Because I am not a hand, I do not belong to the body," that would not make it any less a part of the body. And if the ear would say, "Because I am not an eye, I do not belong to the body," that would not make it any less a part of the body. If the whole body were an eye, where would the hearing be? If the whole body were hearing, where would the sense of smell be? But as it is, God arranged the members in the body, each one of them, as he chose. If all were a single member, where would the body be? As it is, there are many members, yet one body. The eye cannot say to the hand, "I have no need of you," nor again the head to the feet, "I have no need of you." On the contrary, the members of the body that seem to be weaker are indispensable, and those members of the body that we think less honorable we clothe with greater honor, and our less respectable members are treated with greater respect; whereas our more respectable members do not need this. But God has so arranged the body, giving the greater honor to the inferior member, that there may be no dissension within the body, but the members may have the same care for one another. If one member suffers, all suffer together with it; if one member is honored, all rejoice together with it.

1 CORINTHIANS 12:12-26

☞ When the groups have completed their study, they are to underline the gifts of the Spirit mentioned in the following passages (these are underlined for you). After they have done this, call on participants to share with the full group what they have underlined as you write their answers on newsprint or a flip chart. Point out that some of the gifts are named more than once using different words. If any of the gifts are overlooked, identify these and add them to the list. End by sharing the following information with the group.

Now concerning spiritual gifts, brothers and sisters, I do not want you to be uninformed. . . .

Now there are varieties of gifts, but the same Spirit; and there are varieties of services, but the same Lord; and there are varieties of activities, but it is the same God who activates all of them in everyone. To each is given the manifestation of the Spirit for the common good. To one is given through the Spirit the utterance of <u>wisdom</u>, and to another the utterance of <u>knowledge</u> according to the same Spirit, to another <u>faith</u> by the same Spirit, to another gifts of <u>healing</u> by the one Spirit, to another the working of <u>miracles</u>, to another <u>prophecy</u>, to another the <u>discernment</u> of spirits, to another various kinds of <u>tongues</u>, to another the <u>interpretation of tongues</u>. All these are activated by one and the same Spirit, who allots to each one individually just as the Spirit chooses.

1 CORINTHIANS 12:1, 4-11

Now you are the body of Christ and individually members of it. And God has appointed in the church first <u>apostles</u>, second <u>prophets</u>, third <u>teachers</u>; then deeds of <u>power</u>, then gifts of <u>healing</u>, forms of <u>assistance</u>, forms of <u>leadership</u>, various kinds of <u>tongues.</u> Are all <u>apostles</u>? Are all <u>prophets</u>? Are all <u>teachers</u>? Do all work <u>miracles</u>? Do all possess gifts of <u>healing</u>? Do all speak in <u>tongues</u>? Do all <u>interpret</u>? But strive for the greater gifts. And I will show you a still more excellent way.

1 CORINTHIANS 12:27-31

In this last passage, the writer names gifts that come to mind as examples. Not all of the gifts are listed here, nor are the gifts ranked in order of importance. This list reminds us that God calls us to service and gives the gifts necessary to do what needs to be done. The gifts are spiritually given but earthly based. They provide us with the tools we need to do Christ's work on earth. God's gifts are given so that we can share in God's ongoing healing of our broken world.

Responsive Listening Bible Study

1 C O R I N T H I A N S 1 2 : 1 2 - 2 6

The building of the community is the goal of the Spirit's work. In your small group, follow the step-by-step instructions on pages 19-20 to study 1 Corinthians 12:1, 4-31.

For just as the body is one and has many members, and all the members of the body, though many, are one body, so it is with Christ. For in the one Spirit we were all baptized into one body—Jews or Greeks, slaves or free—and we were all made to drink of one Spirit.

Indeed, the body does not consist of one member but of many. If the foot would say, "Because I am not a hand, I do not belong to the body," that would not make it any less a part of the body. And if the ear would say, "Because I am not an eye, I do not belong to the body," that would not make it any less a part of the body. If the whole body were an eye, where would the hearing be? If the whole body were hearing, where would the sense of smell be? But as it is, God arranged the members in the body, each one of them, as he chose. If all were a single member, where would the body be? As it is, there are many members, yet one body. The eye cannot say to the hand, "I have no need of you," nor again the head to the feet, "I have no need of you." On the contrary, the members of the body that seem to be weaker are indispensable, and those members of the body that we think less honorable we clothe with greater honor, and our less respectable members are treated with greater respect; whereas our more respectable members do not need this. But God has so arranged the body, giving the greater honor to the inferior member, that there may be no dissension within the body, but the members may have the same care for one another. If one member suffers, all suffer together with it; if one member is honored, all rejoice together with it.

1 CORINTHIANS 12:12-26

69

When your group has completed the Bible study, locate and underline the gifts of the Holy Spirit named in the following passages. When you have finished, reflect on the passage in silence and wait for further instructions.

> Now concerning spiritual gifts, brothers and sisters, I do not want you to be uninformed. . . .
> Now there are varieties of gifts, but the same Spirit; and there are varieties of services, but the same Lord; and there are varieties of activities, but it is the same God who activates all of them in everyone. To each is given the manifestation of the Spirit for the common good. To one is given through the Spirit the utterance of wisdom, and to another the utterance of knowledge according to the same Spirit, to another faith by the same Spirit, to another gifts of healing by the one Spirit, to another the working of miracles, to another prophecy, to another the discernment of spirits, to another various kinds of tongues, to another the interpretation of tongues. All these are activated by one and the same Spirit, who allots to each one individually just as the Spirit chooses.
>
> 1 CORINTHIANS 12:1, 4-11

> Now you are the body of Christ and individually members of it. And God has appointed in the church first apostles, second prophets, third teachers; then deeds of power, then gifts of healing, forms of assistance, forms of leadership, various kinds of tongues. Are all apostles? Are all prophets? Are all teachers? Do all work miracles? Do all possess gifts of healing? Do all speak in tongues? Do all interpret? But strive for the greater gifts. And I will show you a still more excellent way.
>
> 1 CORINTHIANS 12:27-31

70

The Body of Christ

☞ Display overhead, page 134.
Participant's Workbook page 71.
Have the participants complete their worksheets as you present the material.

1. *The Local Congregation,* as a Part of *the Church,* Is the Body of Christ.

The Body of Christ can refer to all Christians who have lived throughout the ages. In the SpiritGifts program, however, the Body of Christ refers to the community of Christians, the church. We as congregations of the church stand with God and one another in covenant relationship. A covenant is a promise and commitment. This covenant centers on our shared commitment to Jesus Christ and our living and working together as the Body of Christ in the world. As the Body of Christ, we share in ministry with God. Our ministry bonds our relationship between us and God and between us and God's people.

2. When the Body of Christ Works as It Should, It *Strengthens* and *Brings Unity.*

The gifts are given to strengthen and bring unity to the Body of Christ. We respect each member of the body and the gifts he or she brings. Everyone is given certain gifts, but not the same gifts. As we acknowledge and accept the diversity of gifts within the Body of Christ, we begin to think in new ways about the strengths of others. And as we begin to use our gifts within the community, we allow them to be expressed in different ways at different times and we begin to take the crucial step of trusting one another.

3. We Each *Take Our Place* in The Body of Christ.

When we each name, claim, and use our gifts within the congregation, we take our created place within the life of the community. Each one of us has a place within the church to express ourselves as a unique individual who is gifted for ministry. God gives all the gifts needed for ministry so that the body will function as God intends.

4. *Harmony* Comes in the Body of Christ.

Because God distributes the gifts as needed, there is harmony between people and groups within the life of the congregation. Even though there is great diversity in the expressions of the gifts, each of us brings a commitment to the community effort. When used correctly and integrated properly, our diversity is our greatest strength.

5. *Mutual Interdependency* Is Built in the Body of Christ.

As we each use our unique gifts in a variety of ways, we build a healthy mutual interdependence. In a culture that stresses independence and advocates a "loner mentality," this is good news. We don't have to do it on our own. Each of us is needed.

Intimacy grows as we work together. This intimacy and the trust it brings allow us to work with change, deal with conflict, and reach our full potential. Through this intimacy we find an atmosphere of spiritual openness in our relationships, enabling us to tolerate risks and forgive errors.

6. The Congregation Grows When the Body of Christ *Loves and Cares for Its Members.*

Touching is at the heart of who we are as a body. As our lives touch, we experience one another's ups and downs. We share the tragedies and joys of our personal lives, and we touch each other.

Persons outside our community see this love and care and are drawn by the "charisma." With the Holy Spirit, we invite them to join us in Christ. In a congregation where everyone is doing her or his created job, the congregation grows both spiritually and numerically.

The Body of Christ

1. *The local congregation*, as a part of *the church*, is the Body of Christ.

2. When the Body of Christ works as it should, it *strengthens* and *brings unity*.

3. We each *take our place* in the Body of Christ.

4. *Harmony* comes in the Body of Christ.

5. *Mutual interdependency* is built in the Body of Christ.

6. The congregation grows when the Body of Christ *loves and cares for its members*.

The Body of Christ

If you have not already done so, read and reflect on 1 Corinthians 12:12-31. Then complete this worksheet as the leader further clarifies how we are the Body of Christ.

1. _____, as a part of

_____, is the Body of Christ.

2. When the Body of Christ works as it should, it

_____ and _____.

3. We each _____ in the Body of Christ.

4. _____ comes in the Body of Christ.

5. _____ is built in the Body of Christ.

6. The congregation grows when the Body of

Christ _____

_____.

71

I Am a Part of the Body of Christ

👉 *Participant's Workbook* page 72.

Think of the picture on your worksheet as representative of the Body of Christ. According to 1 Corinthians 12, parts of the body represent the wide variety of gifts belonging to persons in the Christian community. We do not play a part in determining our gifts for ministry; they are given by God. Therefore, we cannot compare our gifts with the gifts of others to determine which have greater or lesser value. Just as no single component of our body can claim superiority over another part, all gifts are of equal value.

Jesus demonstrated cooperation in his ministry. So also our work together is one of collegiality. The heart in this picture reminds us that the Spirit of Christ is at the heart as we work in partnership together.

As you look at the picture, consider what part you are in the Body of Christ. Color or circle this part. Then find a partner and tell why you chose this part.

I Am a Part of the Body of Christ

Read 1 Corinthians 12:12-31.

As a part of the Body of Christ pictured here, what part are you? Color or circle it and discuss with another person why you chose this part.

72

Responsive Listening Bible Study

1 CORINTHIANS 13

👉 *Participant's Workbook* page 73.

After Paul speaks extensively about the gifts of the Spirit throughout 1 Corinthians 12, he tells his readers, "But strive for the greater gifts. And I will show you a still more excellent way" (v. 31). The more excellent way that Paul refers to is the way of love. In chapter 13, Paul continues to discuss spiritual gifts. In essence he says that the greatest gift of the Spirit is not tongues or even prophecy; it is love. This love is not love in an ordinary or general sense; it is the love that is known within the church, the very love of God poured out in Christ. Love is not listed in SpiritGifts as a nineteenth gift of the Spirit, because it is clear that the gift of love is a foundational gift that must undergird the use of all the other gifts. God is love. Love is the one gift that all of us must claim as our own.

👉 After reading the preceding introductory comments, have the participants break into small groups and follow the step-by-step instructions for Responsive Listening Bible Study (*Participant's Workbook* pages 19-20, *Leader's Resources* pages 61-62).

During the study, walk from group to group, asking what step the group is on and if they have any questions or concerns. Be attuned to groups who get bogged down and to facilitators who do not keep their groups moving through the steps as described.

If I speak in the tongues of mortals and of angels, but do not have love, I am a noisy gong or a clanging cymbal. And if I have prophetic powers, and understand all mysteries and all knowledge, and if I have all faith, so as to remove mountains, but do not have love, I am nothing. If I give away all my possessions, and if I hand over my body so that I may boast, but do not have love, I gain nothing.

Love is patient; love is kind; love is not envious or boastful or arrogant or rude. It does not insist on its own way; it is not irritable or resentful; it does not rejoice in wrongdoing, but rejoices in the truth. It bears all things, believes all things, hopes all things, endures all things.

Love never ends. But as for prophecies, they will come to an end; as for tongues, they will cease; as for knowledge, it will come to an end. For we know only in part, and we prophesy only in part; but when the complete comes, the partial will come to an end. When I was a child, I spoke like a child, I thought like a child, I reasoned like a child; when I became an adult, I put an end to childish ways. For now we see in a mirror, dimly, but then we will see face to face. Now I know only in part; then I will know fully, even as I have been fully known. And now faith, hope, and love abide, these three; and the greatest of these is love.

1 CORINTHIANS 13

👉 When the groups have completed their study, proceed to *Strive for the Greater Gifts*, page 140.

Responsive Listening Bible Study

1 CORINTHIANS 13

After Paul speaks extensively about the gifts of the Spirit throughout 1 Corinthians 12, he tells his readers, "But strive for the greater gifts. And I will show you a still more excellent way" (v. 31). The more excellent way that Paul refers to is the way of love.

In your small group, follow the step-by-step instructions on pages 19-20 to study the love chapter, 1 Corinthians 13.

If I speak in the tongues of mortals and of angels, but do not have love, I am a noisy gong or a clanging cymbal. And if I have prophetic powers, and understand all mysteries and all knowledge, and if I have all faith, so as to remove mountains, but do not have love, I am nothing. If I give away all my possessions, and if I hand over my body so that I may boast, but do not have love, I gain nothing.

Love is patient; love is kind; love is not envious or boastful or arrogant or rude. It does not insist on its own way; it is not irritable or resentful; it does not rejoice in wrongdoing, but rejoices in the truth. It bears all things, believes all things, hopes all things, endures all things.

Love never ends. But as for prophecies, they will come to an end; as for tongues, they will cease; as for knowledge, it will come to an end. For we know only in part, and we prophesy only in part; but when the complete comes, the partial will come to an end. When I was a child, I spoke like a child, I thought like a child, I reasoned like a child; when I became an adult, I put an end to childish ways. For now we see in a mirror, dimly, but then we will see face to face. Now I know only in part; then I will know fully, even as I have been fully known. And now faith, hope, and love abide, these three; and the greatest of these is love.

1 CORINTHIANS 13

When your group has finished praying (step 8), reflect on the passage in silence and wait for further instructions.

73

Strive for the Greater Gifts

☞ *Participant's Workbook* page 74.

We respect and admire those who have found a "still more excellent way" (1 Corinthians 12:31). They are those persons who live their lives centered in love. We all know people who use their gifts excellently, who center the use of their gifts in love. They live abundantly and with passion. They know God's purpose for their lives and live in that assurance. In all that they do, they bring glory to God. They inspire us to use our own gifts.

☞ Ask the participants to complete their worksheets. Then have them break into small groups or pairs to discuss their reflections. After several minutes, call the entire group back together and have a few volunteers share any insights they gained from the exercise.

Strive for the Greater Gifts

> But strive for the greater gifts. And I will show you a still more excellent way.
>
> 1 CORINTHIANS 12:31

Think of five people, living or dead, who have found a "still more excellent way." These are persons who center the use of their gifts in love, who know God's purpose for their lives and live in that assurance. In all that they do, they bring glory to God. Write their names and why you admire them below.

1.

2.

3.

4.

5.

For reflection: What gifts of the Spirit do you think these persons have within them? Do their gifts reflect your own gifts or others you wish to discern in yourself?

74

Using Our Gifts in Community

☞ Display overhead, page 145.
Participant's Workbook page 75.
The following information will help participants begin to see how the SpiritGifts program can be foundational to the ongoing work of congregational ministry. Instruct the participants to complete their worksheets as you share information. Allow time for questions and discussion as you move through the material. If your church has not already made a congregational commitment to an ongoing SpiritGifts program, this information session may be the beginning of an exciting new possibility.

In Matthew 5:16 we read, "Let your light shine before others, so that they may see your good works and give glory to your Father in heaven." What a wonderful opportunity we have to utilize our gifts for the good of the greater community. As a part of the Body of Christ, we possess the potential to be a uniting, strengthening, harmonious agent of the gospel. We can commit our gifts to be used within the community of Christ and the world for the glory of God. As we use our gifts, our focus should be on the work of the individual glorifying God, and not on the list of tasks to be done. We are ministers with God. What a wonderful gift!

Let us consider some of the exciting things that can happen when we discern and use our gifts in community.

1. The Community Invites Us to *Grow as Disciples by Naming, Claiming, and Using Our Gifts.*

The community of Christ, the church, is not a secular group or business. We are the Spirit-led community of Jesus. Therefore, when we consider the tasks to be done, we should not look at qualifications or job slots. In the past, nominating committees labored many painful hours to find candidates who were willing to do the work. They saw their purpose as recruiting people for predetermined, institutional roles. They placed warm bodies in job slots to keep the institution running—"the way we've always done it." They nominated people according to their capabilities or recruited those who had the time to give.

Today transformation is taking place across the church. Congregations are placing a new emphasis on the growth and development of the membership. Instead of the emphasis being on the institution and its goals, the primary focus is shifting to the formation of disciples and God's purposes for their lives.

Using our gifts as God intended may abolish the nominating committee as we know it. Now we can speak of spiritual gifts and find individuals with the needed gifts who are called to do the work of ministry. In this way the nominating committee becomes a committee to screen groups and individuals for ministry, inviting people to discern and use their gifts. People will be knocking on the committee's door to work! SpiritGifts can help to bring about this exciting change.

Christ Church is one church that recognizes the need for a practical process to mobilize the congregation for ministry. They have renamed their nominating committee the Spiritual Gifts committee and are using SpiritGifts to help members become an active and vital part of the faith community through the study and employment of their gifts. In this model, seven persons are trained to lead the SpiritGifts program. Each leader teaches the course two times, once each year for two years. Recognizing that interests and schedules vary, they offer the program in numerous ways and at different times, including such options as a six-week program on Wednesday nights; a ten-week program on Tuesday mornings; an ongoing adult Sunday school class; a confirmation class; a two-hour session following Sunday worship, "served up" with soup and salad. One SpiritGifts leader even takes the program to shut-ins of the congregation. These at-home members are amazed and pleased that a lay member comes, not to pick up the offering envelope or deliver a tape of the worship service, but to affirm that at whatever age and stage we are in life, God continues to be at work doing God's will through the development of gifts.

When teaching the course for the second time, each primary leader trains another person who will lead the SpiritGifts program the following year.

Another example is Trinity Church. This congregation has done away with their old administrative structure and restrictive style of programming. Members join small groups based on their gifts and present ministries. At the center of the small group gathering is prayer, Bible study, and fellowship. Reflective Listening Bible Study challenges group members to examine their own lives as well as the situations of the world. Based on their study and reflection, members challenge one another to take action. These groups reach out in mission as they use their gifts, calling one another to service and responsibility. Members gain new energy as they strengthen the connection between who they are and what they are doing.

These two congregations and many others are taking a proactive stance to intentionally involve all their members in the ministry of the church, and they are finding that SpiritGifts is a powerful and effective way to do this. Some congregations require all new members to participate in the program in their first year of membership. As new members identify their gifts, they gain a clear idea about how they should be involved. The added bonus is the bonds they establish with other members as they move into the wider congregation.

A number of congregations invite long-term members to participate in SpiritGifts sometime during a two-year period. A committee is responsible for telephoning each member, similar to the way many congregations schedule photography sittings for the pictorial directory. Each person is invited to choose a SpiritGifts program that fits her or his schedule. Through their study, members gain basic teachings that help them function within the congregation, enabling all persons to take their rightful place in ministry within the larger community. This proactive stance involves introverted, shy persons, who often find themselves outside looking in, as well as extroverted persons, who usually get involved on their own.

2. The Community Helps People to *Be Nurtured and to Mature.*

The work of ministry is not set aside for clergy only; it is for all believers, both laity and clergy. The gifts of the Spirit enable laity to claim ownership of the work of ministry. All believers are ministers with special gifts for ministry. We are all valuable workers. We all need to be given the opportunity to develop the full potential of our gifts.

Using our gifts in community nurtures and matures us to a closer walk with God. As we use our gifts in community, we ourselves grow in faith. As we stretch our potential and find contentment in what God is accomplishing through us, we become more of the full, mature persons God intends us to be.

When the community helps us to identify our gifts, we realize that we are cared about as unique persons. We are not simply being used to maintain ongoing institutional goals; there is a genuine concern for the personal development of each one of us. As we sense this esteem, we begin to take seriously our own spiritual formation and growth. By helping us name and claim our gifts for ministry, the congregation is providing a lifelong opportunity for learning and growth. We are renewed both as individuals and as a congregation.

3. The Community Stops the *Power Struggles Between Members and Groups.*

As we have discussed, one gift is not greater than another, only different. Gifts are received, not achieved. Gifts are from God for the encouragement of the community. When each of us is doing the work God has called us to do, there is no hierarchy. No one job is more important than another. We all are fulfilling an important task with the gift assigned as God planned.

Here is an example. Liz agreed to serve as the teacher's assistant to the third grade Sunday school class shortly after joining the congregation. As a new Christian, Liz put in many hours of study. She was happy to work with Julie, a woman who had taught for many years. Liz said, "The first time Julie called and asked me to teach part of the lesson, I was scared. I was worried that I wouldn't tell the Bible story well. But everything turned out fine. Julie served as my terrific assistant for the morning."

Although Liz believes her gift is assisting, she was glad when the opportunity came to teach the class. The experience gave her a clearer understanding of how to be a better classroom helper. Julie tells parents that she and Liz are a team. They function together as members of the Body of Christ.

A second example is Pastor Stine of New Hope Church. Pastor Stine prayerfully calls on God to give him the wisdom to understand the gifts of the Holy Spirit and bring them to light for others. He understands the need for strong pastoral leadership, yet he equally recognizes the need for a style of leadership that strengthens and supports the gifts of others for ministry. Pastor Stine stands firm in who he is as a child of God and is not threatened by another's power or ability. He does not need to control or make people into who he thinks they should be.

Pastor Stine believes wholeheartedly in shared ministry. He trusts and expects the members to take their rightful place in the ministry of the church. He works hard to help persons find their gifts, rather than persuading or manipulating them to fulfill a predetermined agenda. Pastor Stine encourages persons to take small, measurable steps to work toward and accomplish a vision. Often he steps aside and allows members to take responsibility, knowing that not all efforts will succeed—and that's OK.

Using Our Gifts in Community

> "Let your light shine before others, so that they may see your good works and give glory to your Father in heaven."
>
> MATTHEW 5:16

1. The community invites us to *grow as disciples by naming, claiming, and using our gifts.*

2. The community helps us to *be nurtured and to mature.*

3. The community stops the *power struggles between members and groups.*

Using Our Gifts in Community

"Let your light shine before others, so that they may see your good works and give glory to your Father in heaven."

MATTHEW 5:16

1. The community invites us to _____

_____

_____.

We are the Spirit-led community of Jesus. Therefore, when we consider the tasks to be done, we should not be looking at qualifications or job slots.

2. The community helps us to_____

_____

_____.

The gifts of the Spirit enable all persons to claim ownership of the work of ministry.

3. The community stops the _____

_____

_____.

Gifts are received, not achieved. When each of us is doing the work God has called us to do, there is no hierarchy.

75

Responsive Listening Bible Study

ROMANS 12:3-8

☞ *Participant's Workbook* page 76.
This Bible study is best used as the participants continue to consider their gifts in relationship to the community of believers.

Apparently the early church had members who possessed special or showy gifts and thought this made them better than others. Romans 12:3-8 is Paul's response to this attitude.

☞ Have the participants break into small groups and follow the step-by-step instructions for Responsive Listening Bible Study (*Participant's Workbook* pages 19-20, *Leader's Resources* pages 61-62). During the study, walk from group to group, asking what step the group is on and if they have any questions or concerns. Be attuned to groups who get bogged down and to facilitators who do not keep their groups moving through the steps as described. You may need to remind groups who finish before the others to pray silently for those who are still sharing.

For by the grace given to me I say to everyone among you not to think of yourself more highly than you ought to think, but to think with sober judgment, each according to the measure of faith that God has assigned. For as in one body we have many members, and not all the members have the same function, so we, who are many, are one body in Christ, and individually we are members one of another. We have gifts that differ according to the grace given to us: <u>prophecy</u>, in proportion to faith; <u>ministry</u>, in ministering; the <u>teacher</u>, in teaching; the <u>exhorter</u>, in exhortation; the <u>giver</u>, in generosity; the <u>leader</u>, in diligence; the <u>compassionate</u>, in cheerfulness.

ROMANS 12:3-8

☞ When all the groups have finished their study, call the participants back together and direct them to identify and underline the seven gifts named in the passage (these are underlined for you). Call on participants to share what they have underlined as you write their answers on newsprint, or chalkboard, or a flip chart. If any of the gifts are overlooked, identify these and add them to the list. End with a brief time of sharing in which participants reflect on what they have gained from the experience.

Responsive Listening Bible Study

R O M A N S   1 2 : 3 - 8

Apparently the early church had members who possessed special or showy gifts and thought this made them better than others. Romans 12:3-8 is Paul's response to this attitude. In your small group, follow the step-by-step instructions on pages 19-20 to study this passage.

> For by the grace given to me I say to everyone among you not to think of yourself more highly than you ought to think, but to think with sober judgment, each according to the measure of faith that God has assigned. For as in one body we have many members, and not all the members have the same function, so we, who are many, are one body in Christ, and individually we are members one of another. We have gifts that differ according to the grace given to us: prophecy, in proportion to faith; ministry, in ministering; the teacher, in teaching; the exhorter, in exhortation; the giver, in generosity; the leader, in diligence; the compassionate, in cheerfulness.
>
> ROMANS 12:3-8

When your group has completed the Bible study, locate and underline the seven gifts named in the above passage. When you have finished, reflect on the passage in silence and wait for further instructions.

76

Naming One Another's Gifts

☞ *Participant's Workbook* pages 77-78.
This group-building exercise gives participants the opportunity to affirm one another's gifts. It also emphasizes once again that God's gifts for our lives cannot be discovered or used in isolation, but only in community with others.

You are not journeying through SpiritGifts alone. Others are making the journey with you. With these persons you have studied the gifts of the Spirit; you have thoughtfully considered their gifts and your own; you have talked and listened to one another; you have shared stories about your past; you have talked about future dreams; you have even talked about the people who have inspired your life. You have spoken the truth to one another in love.

This exercise gives your fellow participants the opportunity and awesome task to identify and affirm the gifts they see evidenced in your life. It also gives you the opportunity to affirm the gifts you see in others.

☞ Ask each participant to write her or his name in the space provided on the worksheet and place the worksheet on the table. Then have the participants rise and move from one person's worksheet to another, writing their comments in the space provided, until they have written on three persons' worksheets. As time allows, invite the participants to sit down with those who have written on their worksheets, one at a time, and discuss their comments.

Another option is to provide a colorfully wrapped gift box for each participant (or ask the participants to bring these from home). Each box should have a participant's name written on it and an opening cut in the top of the box. Instruct each participant to choose three people and identify a gift evidenced in the life of each person. For each gift, have the participant write comments on a slip of paper explaining why he or she affirms this gift. After the participants have placed their slips of paper in the proper boxes, let them open their boxes and read the affirmations of their gifts.

Naming One Another's Gifts

You are not journeying through SpiritGifts alone. Others are making the journey with you. With these persons you have studied the gifts of the Spirit; you have thoughtfully considered their gifts and your own; you have talked and listened to one another; you have shared stories about your past; you have talked about future dreams; you have even talked about the people who have inspired your life. You have spoken the truth to one another in love.

This exercise gives you and your fellow participants the opportunity and awesome task to identify and affirm the gifts you see evidenced in one another's lives.

WRITE YOUR NAME HERE: _____

When instructed, rise and move to write on the worksheets of three other participants. There is space to name up to three gifts for each of the three individuals you choose.

1. Writer's name: _____

   Gift(s) I see in you: _____

   _____

   _____

   Reasons I affirm this (these) gift(s):_____

   _____

   _____

   _____

   _____

77

150

2. Writer's name: _____

   Gift(s) I see in you: _____

                     _____

                     _____

   Reasons I affirm this (these) gift(s):_____

_____

_____

_____

_____

_____

3. Writer's name: _____

   Gift(s) I see in you: _____

                     _____

                     _____

   Reasons I affirm this (these) gift(s):_____

_____

_____

_____

_____

78

LEADER

A Passion for God's Purpose

☞ *Participant's Workbook* page 79.

☞ This exercise may require more time for individual reflection than some of the other Spirit-Gifts exercises. You may choose to have participants complete the worksheet at home and bring it with them to the next session. Or you may choose to suggest that participants list fewer responses, perhaps three to five. Either way, allow the participants to complete the exercise before sharing the following comments.

Have you ever thought or felt that church has a lot to do with "Christian duty" and little to do with your own spiritual journey? Many people feel that church is where we are supposed to go to learn how to "be good." Sometimes it seems that the congregation devotes more energy to sustaining programs than to helping us grow spiritually. Sometimes we leave a worship service feeling like we've been given more burdens than good news.

Well, hear this good news! The church is not about "duty"; it is about passion! Duty brings to mind those demands on our time and energy that must be fulfilled even when our heart is elsewhere. But when we work from our passion, we bring vital energy and our very best work to the ministry placed before us.

The church is calling forth the essence of who we are, which is best expressed as we use our unique gifts to live out God's purpose and will for our lives. As we do this, we also call forth the gifts in others. In this way, as individuals and as the church, we experience new energy, new life, and a new sense of purpose and freedom.

Throughout SpiritGifts we have used several different approaches to discern our gifts. Another approach that can provide helpful insights is to identify those things that burn within you and give your life meaning. These might be things that give you passion to live, restore your energy, and call forth the best in you. When you do these things, you feel alive and free; you know that you are living in God's will and that life has meaning. Often those things we are most passionate about reveal where God is calling us to be in ministry. When we live God's purpose for our lives, we know it by the passion with which we pursue it.

What do we mean when we talk about living in God's will? Living in God's will means being in tune with the heart of God. Finding God's will and purpose for our lives is not some mysterious path that only the most pious can walk. Living in God's will is not choosing between "door number one" and "door number two" and "door number three." It is not believing that only one of the doors is truly God's path for us. It is not believing that there is one perfect mate or vocation or calling, and that if we don't find it our life will be forever out of rhythm.

Living in God's will means that as we live our lives, with whatever choices we make or whatever twists and turns we find along our path, we are in touch with God. Living in God's will does not hinge on any title, role, or position we undertake. It cannot be measured by successes or failures as defined by the world. Mary the mother of Jesus was the supreme example of being in tune with the heart of God when she sang, as recorded in Luke 1:47, "My soul magnifies the Lord, and my spirit rejoices in God my Savior." Like Mary, we can live in God's will.

☞ After sharing the preceding comments, ask the participants to break into pairs and discuss the responses on their worksheets. End with a time of sharing with the whole group.

A Passion for God's Purpose

List ten things that burn within you and give your life meaning. These might be the things that give you passion to live, restore your energy, and call forth the best in you. When you do these things, you feel alive and free. You know that you are living in God's will and your life has meaning.

1. _____

2. _____

3. _____

4. _____

5. _____

6. _____

7. _____

8. _____

9. _____

10. _____

What clues, if any, does this list give you about your gifts? What patterns emerge? Discuss this with a partner and with the whole group as time allows.

79

Responsive Listening Bible Study

MATTHEW 7:15-20; GALATIANS 5:22-25

☞ *Participant's Workbook* page 80.

Have the participants break into small groups and follow the step-by-step instructions for Responsive Listening Bible Study (*Participant's Workbook* pages 19-20, *Leader's Resources* pages 61-62), reading both texts each time the instructions call for an oral reading. During the study, walk from group to group, asking what step the group is on and if they have any questions or concerns. Be attuned to groups who get bogged down and to facilitators who do not keep their groups on track. Before the groups begin, tell them that they are to underline the nine fruits of the Spirit mentioned in the passage from Galatians when they have completed their study (these are underlined for you).

"Beware of false prophets, who come to you in sheep's clothing but inwardly are ravenous wolves. You will know them by their fruits. Are grapes gathered from thorns, or figs from thistles? In the same way, every good tree bears good fruit, but the bad tree bears bad fruit. A good tree cannot bear bad fruit, nor can a bad tree bear good fruit. Every tree that does not bear good fruit is cut down and thrown into the fire. Thus you will know them by their fruits."

MATTHEW 7:15-20

By contrast, the fruit of the Spirit is <u>love</u>, <u>joy</u>, <u>peace</u>, <u>patience</u>, <u>kindness</u>, <u>generosity</u>, <u>faithfulness</u>, <u>gentleness</u>, and <u>self-control</u>. There is no law against such things. And those who belong to Christ Jesus have crucified the flesh with its passions and desires. If we live by the Spirit, let us also be guided by the Spirit.

GALATIANS 5:22-25

Responsive Listening Bible Study

MATTHEW 7:15-20; GALATIANS 5:22-25

In your small group, follow the step-by-step instructions on pages 19-20 to study these two passages that teach us about the fruit of the Spirit. Read both texts each time the instructions call for an oral reading.

> "Beware of false prophets, who come to you in sheep's clothing but inwardly are ravenous wolves. You will know them by their fruits. Are grapes gathered from thorns, or figs from thistles? In the same way, every good tree bears good fruit, but the bad tree bears bad fruit. A good tree cannot bear bad fruit, nor can a bad tree bear good fruit. Every tree that does not bear good fruit is cut down and thrown into the fire. Thus you will know them by their fruits."
>
> MATTHEW 7:15-20

> By contrast, the fruit of the Spirit is love, joy, peace, patience, kindness, generosity, faithfulness, gentleness, and self-control. There is no law against such things. And those who belong to Christ Jesus have crucified the flesh with its passions and desires. If we live by the Spirit, let us also be guided by the Spirit.
>
> GALATIANS 5:22-25

When your group has completed its study, refer back to the passage from Galatians and underline the nine fruits that are named as evidences of the Spirit's indwelling presence.

80

Evidences of Our Gifts Are Found in "Fruits"

☞ One of the common questions persons ask when studying the gifts of the Holy Spirit is "How are the gifts different from the fruit of the Spirit?" The following material serves as a good response to this question as well as an introduction to two New Testament passages that teach us about the fruit of the Spirit.

The basic test to determine if someone is filled with the Spirit is to look at the person's life. How is the person employing her or his gifts? We know a gift is from God when the gift is employed in concrete, loving ways. The Bible calls these evidences the "fruit of the Spirit." Jesus says that we can distinguish between good people and bad people by their "fruits," or what their actions produce:

> "Beware of false prophets, who come to you in sheep's clothing but inwardly are ravenous wolves. You will know them by their fruits. Are grapes gathered from thorns, or figs from thistles? In the same way, every good tree bears good fruit, but the bad tree bears bad fruit. A good tree cannot bear bad fruit, nor can a bad tree bear good fruit. Every tree that does not bear good fruit is cut down and thrown into the fire. Thus you will know them by their fruits."
>
> MATTHEW 7:15-20

In this passage, taken from Jesus' Sermon on the Mount, Jesus expounds on the Golden Rule stated earlier in the sermon. Though the passage talks specifically about false prophets, the observation can be applied to other actions as well. Jesus is saying that not only our actions are important but also what results from our actions. We all have done things, with the best intentions, that have gone wrong. When a person lives out of his or her gifts, intentions are lived out in rightful actions. God's plan is actualized. Fruits grow and develop as we walk in obedience to the Spirit of God. Fruits are the end result of living God's will through the use of our gifts.

We also read in the Bible that faith produces good works—the fruit of the Spirit—through love:

> By contrast, the fruit of the Spirit is love, joy, peace, patience, kindness, generosity, faithfulness, gentleness, and self-control. There is no law against such things. And those who belong to Christ Jesus have crucified the flesh with its passions and desires. If we live by the Spirit, let us also be guided by the Spirit. Let us not become conceited, competing against one another, envying one another.
>
> GALATIANS 5:22-26

This passage from Galatians stresses that loving service is life in the Spirit. The writer, Paul, asserts that Christians must be open to the Spirit's leading. The Spirit is the ruling power in the Christian's life. Paul is interested in practical application and good results for community life.

The last sentence, verse 26, reflects the division and disharmony that occur when gifts are used for our own self-centeredness and divisive pride. Gifts of the Spirit are to be centered in love and respect for ourselves, our neighbors, and all of creation. The spirit of love brings harmony and unity. When we prayerfully serve God's people in concrete, constructive ways, we work out of the qualities of love, joy, peace, kindness, generosity, faithfulness, gentleness, and self-control. With each step we grow in Christian maturity. As we radiate the fruit of the Spirit, we are effective witnesses of God's love in the world.

Getting Ready to Use Your Gifts

☞ Display overhead, page 160.
Participant's Workbook page 81.
Have the participants complete their worksheets as you present the following information.

Now that you have used several different methods and tools to name, claim, and understand your gifts, consider these four important steps for getting ready to use your gifts.

1. Get Ready to Use Each Gift Through *Spiritual Preparation.*

You can prepare yourself to use each gift given to you to its greatest advantage for the work of God. Exposing yourself to opportunities to use your gift will strengthen not only your ability but also your confidence to use the gift more and more. Develop your gift so that it can be cultivated to its greatest potential. You must be unreservedly willing to do the things that you know will make the fullest use of each of your spiritual gifts. Translating your faith into action is the objective.

In order to remain open to God's opportunities, you will want to continue to grow in the spiritual practices that keep you centered in Christ and in right relationship with God. These practices, sometimes referred to as spiritual disciplines, differ for each person. Whatever practices you employ, the basics will include prayer and reflection, Bible reading and study, and Christian fellowship that supports and calls you to responsibility.

2. Accept *Responsibility* for Your Gifts.

After naming your gifts, you are responsible for using them within the life of the community to further the work of Jesus. Let others know of your gifts so that they may call upon you when opportunities arise for your gifts. As your church community looks ahead, they can incorporate you into the planned ministries. Since your community knows what gifts are available from you and others, they can plan in ways that best utilize members' gifts. Your church may not wish to have a healing ministry if no one has the gift of healing. But the church may choose to have a strong ministry of teaching if a number of members have the gift of teaching.

3. *Get to Work.*

Find tangible ways to use your gifts in ministry. As you exercise and use your gifts, you will grow in their proficiency. Faithful utilization of your gifts brings increased effectiveness. When you are engaged in the areas in which you are gifted, you will discover that your work is no longer a burden but an exciting, passion-filled adventure. You will have new energy for the work. Incorporate using your gifts in every facet of your life: at work, at home, in your recreational activities, as well as within the Body of Christ, the church.

4. Be Open to *God's Will in Your Life.*

Time and time again you will see that when God wants something to be done, people are equipped with corresponding gifts so that they can get the job done. Be open to God acting in your life in new and unexpected ways. If you desire a gift, don't be afraid to ask God for it. Desire expressed through prayer may lead to the existence of the gift. Of course, just because you desire a gift does not guarantee that you'll get it. Instead, you must place yourself in God's will, knowing that God leads the way. When you do this, your desire and God's desire become one.

Most important, share all of this with God through prayer. Ask God to help you find courage to act on what you have discerned about your gifts.

Getting Ready to Use Your Gifts

How do you get ready to use your gifts?

1. Get ready to use each gift through *spiritual preparation*.

2. Accept *responsibility* for your gifts.

3. *Get to work.*

4. Be open to *God's will in your life*.

Most important, share all this with God through prayer. Ask God to help you find the courage to act on what you have discerned about your gifts.

Getting Ready to Use Your Gifts

How do you get ready to use your gifts?

1. Get ready to use each gift through _____

_____.

2. Accept _____ for your gifts.

3. _____.

4. Be open to _____

_____.

Most important, share all this with God through prayer. Ask God to help you find the courage to act on what you have discerned about your gifts.

81

A Quick Inventory

☞ *Participant's Workbook* page 82.

This quick inventory provides an opportunity for each of you to assess the gifts that you have discerned and are willing to name and claim as your own. It encourages you to evaluate ways you are presently using your gifts as well as envision ways you might use your gifts in the future.

☞ Ask the participants to follow the instructions on the worksheet to complete a quick inventory. After they have done this, have them break into small groups. One at a time, group members are to name one of their gifts and tell (1) how they presently see themselves using this gift and (2) what prayerful hopes and dreams they have for using the gift in the future.

A Quick Inventory

In the column on the left, list the gifts that you have discerned and are willing to name and claim as your own. In the middle column, list the ways you are presently using each gift. In the column on the right, list concrete, tangible ways you envision yourself living out these gifts in the future.

Gift	Present Uses	Future Uses

When instructed, join others in a small group. One at a time, name one of your gifts and tell (1) how you presently use the gift and (2) what prayerful hopes and dreams you have for using the gift in the future.

82

A Blessed Healing

All of us have had disappointments, heartaches, deep wounds, and difficult seasons in our lives. We also have experienced healings, bindings of our spirits, and seasons of refreshment.

It is because we have felt and known the healing touch of God in our own lives that we have the confidence to undertake anything in the name of Jesus. It is because we know that God has been faithful and has kept God's promises that we have the strength and courage to keep on when difficult times return. We also remember those persons who came into our lives during these times of distress. These are the people who ministered to us. They brought light in the midst of darkness and relief in the midst of anguish.

Buried in the stories of our healings, of how we once again found wholeness, is what God might be calling us to do. From these stories we can gain some understanding of God's will and purpose for our lives. In these stories we can begin to see how others have used their gifts—whether known or unknown to them—to serve the greater good. In these recollections of our own lives we can see how God is at work, using our giftedness for God's purpose.

Listen to Sally's story. Sally, a divorced woman with a two-year-old child, came to midweek Bible study in tears. Since the divorce, the father of her child had been absent from their lives. Now a successful business woman, she was married to a man whose work required him to spend weeks at a time on the road. She alone was fully responsible for her preschooler.

"I felt abandoned at the time," Sally shared a year later. "Thankfully, Mary Ann, a friend from my Bible study group, drank a lot of coffee with me during that difficult time. I don't know what I would have done without her sympathetic ear and box of tissues." Sally and Mary Ann, also a divorced mother, with two children, decided to start a support group for single parents. They wanted to share the healing of Christ with others.

☞ *Participant's Workbook* page 83.

Take a few minutes to reflect on experiences in which you found healing and wholeness in the midst of brokenness. Remember also the times you were blessed when you reached out to someone in a difficult season of his or her life. Write about these experiences on your worksheet. This will help you to think about your own healing as well as how you are present in others' healing. It also will give you new understanding for how you might use your gifts in ministry with others.

☞ After the participants have completed their worksheets, have them share their responses in pairs and then with the full group as time allows.

A Blessed Healing

Reflect on experiences when you have found healing and wholeness in the midst of brokenness. Remember also the times you have been blessed when you reached out to someone in a difficult season of his or her life. Think about your own healing as well as how you aided others in their need for healing. Write about these experiences in the space below.

Does your experience give you any understanding of how you might use your gifts in ministry with others? Make notes below:

Share your reflections with another person or with the group as time allows.

83

Responsive Listening Bible Study

> ☞ *Participant's Workbook* page 84.
>
> As you begin to bring your SpiritGifts program to a close, Acts 1 helps participants understand how Jesus prepared his disciples for the close of one chapter in their relationship and the opening of a new one. In this passage are recorded some of Jesus' final instructions to his followers.
>
> Have the participants break into small groups and follow the step-by-step instructions for Responsive Listening Bible Study (*Participant's Workbook* pages 19-20, *Leader's Resources* pages 61-62). As you have done previously, walk from group to group during the study, asking what step the group is on and if they have any questions or concerns. Be attuned to groups who get bogged down and to facilitators who do not keep their groups on track. Before the groups begin, instruct them to remain silent after they have finished praying (step 8) and to wait for further instructions.

The book of Acts continues the narrative of Luke's Gospel by tracing the story of the Christian movement from the resurrection of Jesus to the time when the apostle Paul was preaching in Rome. Theophilus means "lover of God" and might refer to any reader who loves God. The first Christians waited in an attitude of expectant hope, and they were not disappointed.

> In the first book, Theophilus, I wrote about all that Jesus did and taught from the beginning until the day when he was taken up to heaven, after giving instructions through the Holy Spirit to the apostles whom he had chosen. After his suffering he presented himself alive to them by many convincing proofs, appearing to them during forty days and speaking about the kingdom of God. While staying with them, he ordered them not to leave Jerusalem, but to wait there for the promise of the Father. "This," he said, "is what you have heard from me; for John baptized with water, but you will be baptized with the Holy Spirit not many days from now."
>
> So when they had come together, they asked him, "Lord, is this the time when you will restore the kingdom to Israel?" He replied, "It is not for you to know the times or periods that the Father has set by his own authority. But you will receive power when the Holy Spirit has come upon you; and you will be my witnesses in Jerusalem, in all Judea and Samaria, and to the ends of the earth."
>
> ACTS 1:1-8

Responsive Listening Bible Study

The book of Acts continues the narrative of Luke's Gospel by tracing the story of the Christian movement from the resurrection of Jesus to the time when the apostle Paul was preaching in Rome. Theophilus means "lover of God" and might refer to any reader who loves God. The first Christians waited in an attitude of expectant hope, and they were not disappointed.

In your small group, follow the step-by-step instructions on pages 19-20 to study Acts 1:1-8.

In the first book, Theophilus, I wrote about all that Jesus did and taught from the beginning until the day when he was taken up to heaven, after giving instructions through the Holy Spirit to the apostles whom he had chosen. After his suffering he presented himself alive to them by many convincing proofs, appearing to them during forty days and speaking about the kingdom of God. While staying with them, he ordered them not to leave Jerusalem, but to wait there for the promise of the Father. "This," he said, "is what you have heard from me; for John baptized with water, but you will be baptized with the Holy Spirit not many days from now."

So when they had come together, they asked him, "Lord, is this the time when you will restore the kingdom to Israel?" He replied, "It is not for you to know the times or periods that the Father has set by his own authority. But you will receive power when the Holy Spirit has come upon you; and you will be my witnesses in Jerusalem, in all Judea and Samaria, and to the ends of the earth."

ACTS 1:1-8

When your group has finished praying (step 8), reflect on the passage in silence and wait for further instructions.

84

Guided Prayer: Breathing in the Holy Spirit

☞ This guided prayer exercise is best used at the end of a session or immediately before taking a scheduled break. You will need recorded "mood music" of at least ten minutes in duration. The music should be an instrumental selection that is unrecognized by the participants, so that they are not distracted by words or a familiar tune. Play the recording very softly to filter out any distracting sounds or "white noise" in the room.

Make sure there will be no interruptions during the exercise. Dim the lights. Then ask the participants to empty their hands and laps and assume a comfortable, relaxed position. If they are sitting at tables, suggest they push their chairs back from the tables so that there is space around them. Some persons may want to sit or lie on the floor. The objective is for the participants to get as comfortable as the environment allows.

The experience will be most effective if you read at a relaxed pace and with a strong but soft voice.

The Prayer

I'd like you to be as comfortable as you can be. Close your eyes and allow your body to relax. Begin a slow, rhythmic pattern of breathing. As you breathe in, imagine the Holy Spirit entering through every pore of your body. Breathe in (pause); now exhale. Breathe in (pause); and exhale. Relax your feet on the floor. Let the tension go. Feel your back rubbing against your clothing as you breathe in and out. Your arms and hands are relaxed in your lap or at your sides. Allow your neck muscles to relax. Feel the tension escape from the back of your head to your face. Now feel the tension go from your eyes, eyebrows, cheeks, mouth, and jaw. Breathe in (pause); breathe out.

As you sit and wait, there is a gentle warmth pouring over you, surrounding you and caressing you. The love of the Spirit, God's Spirit, is pouring into you, filling the center of your being. The soft wind of the Spirit's presence surrounds and fills your every pore, enveloping you with a love and warmth that is caring, gentle. You breathe in (pause) that love (pause), that peace. The Spirit's presence is strongly felt (pause)—Spirit as friend, caretaker, comforter, loving presence.

Now the gentle Spirit invites Jesus to come. Jesus emerges and, one with the Spirit, kneels at your feet. Appearing before you as one, they wash and caress your feet with oil and tears. You feel the freedom of their caress. They caress gently, touching each of your wounds—those places in yourself that you hold back, those places that hurt the most. Gently, soothingly—healing and embracing. Breathe in (pause); breathe out. And as you breathe out, you do not lose Jesus' presence but carry the healing balm deep within you, to the core of your being.

As you sit enwrapped with the Spirit, imagine energy rising up from your feet and pulsating through you—through your toes and heels (pause), through your calves and thighs (pause), through your buttocks (pause), through the bottom of your spine and into your back (pause), through your lungs (pause), and up through the back of your neck.

Now feel Jesus place his hands on your head. Breathe in and look into Jesus' eyes. As you exhale, imagine God's love flowing through you. As you feel the Spirit's presence, let your body be warmed and filled. Allow the Spirit to hold you, embracing you in the warmth for a moment longer.

As you are ready, begin to return. You know it is time to return. You know that Jesus is still with you, even as you are returning. You feel the Spirit's light radiating, warming you from your center. You remain rested and assured. Your time centered with the Spirit was good, and you will be able to make the journey again another time. When you are ready, mentally return to the room and open your eyes.

☞ After concluding the prayer, allow the room to remain quiet and participants to engage with you and the group as they are ready to do so. When everyone has mentally returned to the room, share the peace of Christ by saying, "The peace of Christ be with you all," to which they may respond, "And also with you." Then say to the group, "As you prepare to leave, I invite you to share the peace of Christ and to affirm one another with a greeting, such as a handshake or a hug, as is appropriate."

Claiming Your Gifts for Ministry

 Participant's Workbook page 85.
In this exercise, participants will
- summarize their gifts,
- deal with any reservations they feel about a particular gift they have discerned,
- share any concerns with members of the group.

The worksheet gives participants the opportunity to summarize their work to this point. Ask them to complete the worksheet individually. Then invite participants to share with the group as they are comfortable. Stress that naming our gifts before one another is important so that we can begin to use our gifts purposefully and responsibly in community.

After the group has shared responses, break into small groups. Create intimate settings by having each group place their chairs in a circle. Instruct the persons in each group to take turns answering this question: "What would I like other members of the group to remember in prayer as I continue to seek to know and live God's will for my life?"

Stress that group members are not to give verbal feedback. This is a time for listening; it is not a time for group members to talk among themselves. After each person has finished sharing, the group is to pray with that person before moving on to the next person. Encourage each group to do this in the way that is most comfortable for them. Suggest that they may want to join hands. Or, with the individual's permission, they may lay hands upon the person for the time of prayer. Each person in the group may take a turn praying for the individual, or one person may be designated to pray. The group members are to continue sharing and praying until all who wish to speak have had the opportunity.

As the leader, feel free to adapt this exercise as you find helpful.

Claiming Your Gifts for Ministry

1. List the gifts that you have named and claimed through the personal survey and study process of the SpiritGifts program.

2. List the gifts that other members of your group have affirmed in you.

3. Name the gift you feel most comfortable with and tell why.

4. Name the gift you feel least comfortable with and tell why.

5. Complete the following statement:
   These are some of the ways I may live God's will for my life using my gifts:

6. What would you like the other members of your group to remember in prayer as you continue to seek to know and live God's will for your life?

85

A Letter to My Congregation

☞ *Participant's Workbook* page 86.

The purpose of this letter is to help you name and claim your gifts for use in the context of the larger faith community. By completing this letter, you take the important step of informing others of your gifts and your place in the Body of Christ.

Under "My gifts that I have identified are," list the gifts that you have identified and *claimed* as your own. Perhaps you have identified gifts that you are not willing or ready to claim for various reasons. Do not include these.

Under "In the past I have been involved in the following types of ministries," list the ministries that you have been involved in within the congregation as well as the greater community. These involvements may relate directly to your church or to your occupation, hobbies, or community volunteer services.

Under "In the future I would like to be involved in the following types of ministries," list the ministries that hold current interest for you and that match the gifts you have named and claimed. Items from the previous statements also may be included here.

When you are finished, sign and date the letter in the spaces provided.

☞ Collect the letters before the participants leave the final session.

The participants' letters can be used in a number of ways:

- Give the letters to the spiritual gifts committee or the program planning group of the congregation. They may use the information as they consider the mission and ministries of the congregation.
- Share the letters with the nominating committee, with the understanding that the information is not to be used to "slot" people into predetermined positions. Instead, the committee should use the letters to determine how the individuals see themselves in ministry and then aid and support them in the use of their gifts.
- Invite participants to form small groups that cluster persons of compatible gifts for mission. For example, a number of persons with the gift of assisting might work to establish a food bank or another mission project.
- Display the letters on a bulletin board to be shared with the congregation. Read them during a congregational gathering or as part of the worship service offering. This enables members to network with one another for ministry.

However you decide to use the letters, be sure to tell the participants of your plans and to ask for their permission. They need to have a clear understanding of the purpose of the letters and know what to expect.

A Letter to My Congregation

Dear Friends,

I have taken part in the SpiritGifts program, along with other members of this congregation. Together we have studied, worked, and prayed to discern the gifts of the Spirit that God has given us for ministry. We understand that these gifts are not to be kept to ourselves, but are to be shared within the community, the Body of Christ. In this way we can take our needed places and live God's will and purpose for our lives.

My gifts that I have identified are:

In the past I have been involved in the following types of ministries:

In the future I would like to be involved in the following types of ministries:

_____
(Signature)

_____
(Date)

86

Certificate of Completion

☞ Make a copy of the Certificate of Completion for each participant (*Leader's Resources* page 175). Be sure to choose a quality paper stock that reproduces well.

Giving each participant a Certificate of Completion at the conclusion of the SpiritGifts program gives the individual a feeling of satisfaction in completing the program. It also establishes a way for the congregation and its leaders to acknowledge and value the time and energy the participant has put into the program. Presenting the certificate at a Sunday worship service during the offering time, immediately before Holy Communion, or at another major congregational worship time stresses to others that this is important. It says, "The SpiritGifts program is an important part of what we do and who we are."

The presentation of the certificate also raises the interest of those who have not yet participated in SpiritGifts. You may want to have one or two of the participants share a short witness about how SpiritGifts has affected them. Let visitors and other attendees know that after the service there will be someone at an information booth or a particular place in the building to give further information about SpiritGifts, including how to sign up for the program.

Another option is to present the certificates at the end of the final SpiritGifts session as part of the *SpiritGifts Covenant and Renewal Service* (pages 176-80). Create a worship celebration. It would be most appropriate to celebrate Holy Communion if time allows.

For either presentation, you may choose to use the blessing found on pages 177-78.

Certificate of Completion

This certifies that

has completed the SpiritGifts program and has made a commitment to name, claim, and use the spiritual gifts listed below in ministry according to God's will.

_____
Pastor   *Date*

_____
SpiritGifts Leader

I believe my spiritual gifts are:

I will use these gifts in the following ministries:

_____
Participant   *Date*

SpiritGifts Covenant and Renewal Service

☞ This covenant and renewal service may be used with participants at the end of the Spirit-Gifts program or in a larger gathering of the congregation.

Opening Song

"Many Gifts, One Spirit" (*Leader's Resources* pages 46-47; *Participant's Workbook* pages 12-13).

Opening Words

Our Living God, Eternal Spirit, has sustained us, strengthened us, and brought us to this day. We give thanks for the Spirit's rich blessings that fill our lives.

The Spirit moves us to love and challenge one another.
The Spirit empowers us with patience, courage, and wisdom.
The Spirit gives us good and varied gifts to be the church in ministry to the world.

We now name our gifts, acknowledge Christ's claim on our lives, and live with renewed boldness as the Body of Christ.

Prayer

Spirit of God, move within us so that we will be your witness to the world. Move among us, binding us together in love. Move through us, making us channels of God's love. Amen.

Scripture

In the first book, Theophilus, I wrote about all that Jesus did and taught from the begining until the day when he was taken up to heaven, after giving instructions through the Holy Spirit to the apostles whom he had chosen. After his suffering he presented himself alive to them by many convincing proofs, appearing to them during forty days and speaking about the kingdom of God. While staying with them, he ordered them not to leave Jerusalem, but to wait there for the promise of the Father. "This," he said, "is what you have heard from me; for John baptized with water, but you will be baptized with the Holy Spirit not many days from now."

So when they had come together, they asked him, "Lord, is this the time when you will restore the kingdom to Israel?" He replied, "It is not for you to know the times or periods that the Father has set by his own authority. But you will receive power when the Holy Spirit has come upon you; and you will be my witnesses in Jerusalem, in all Judea and Samaria, and to the ends of the earth."

ACTS 1:1-8

Reflective Comments on Scripture

 Invite each participant to respond to the following questions using an "I" statement.
- From what I have heard and shared, what does God want me to do or be this week?
- How does God invite me to change?

Certificate Presentation

 The certificates should be completed and signed before the service. Call each participant by name and present the certificate as you say the following.

Leader: (Name), receive this certificate as a gifted child of God.

Participants: (Name), we recognize God's gifts in you and pray for the Holy Spirit's guidance upon you to live God's will all the days of your life.

The Blessing

 Instruct each person to find a partner and pause. If someone is without a partner, you may invite the person to join you. Then give the following directions.

Turn and face each other. The blessing will be shared two times. Decide which one of you will be the giver of the blessing and which one will be the receiver of the blessing the first time. (Pause.)

You will then switch roles, and I will repeat the blessing a second time. We use the mark of the cross, a symbol used by the earliest Christians, to mark the blessing of the Holy Spirit upon our lives. The mark of the cross is made by tracing the cross upon the person with your thumb print. Watch as I demonstrate.

 Demonstrate by placing the mark upon the forehead of one of the participants.

Trace the cross upon each part of the body as it is mentioned. Those receiving the mark may respond by saying amen. Let us practice saying amen. (Pause and wait for participants to say amen.)

There is nothing else you need to say, and you do not repeat.

LEADER: Receive the blessing of the Spirit upon your forehead. May this sign strengthen you in peace and love.

THOSE GATHERED: Amen.

LEADER: Receive the blessing of the Spirit upon your ears. May you hear the gospel of Christ, the Word of life.

THOSE GATHERED: Amen.

LEADER: Receive the blessing of the Spirit upon your eyes. May the light of Christ illumine your way.

THOSE GATHERED: Amen.

LEADER: Receive the blessing of the Spirit upon your lips. May you sing praises to Christ all your days.

THOSE GATHERED: Amen.

LEADER: Receive the blessing of the Spirit upon your heart. May God's Spirit dwell there by faith.

THOSE GATHERED: Amen.

LEADER: Receive the blessing of the Spirit upon your shoulders. May you bear the yoke of Christ with patience and perseverance.

THOSE GATHERED: Amen.

LEADER: Receive the blessing of the Spirit upon your hands. May God's mercy be known in your works.

THOSE GATHERED: Amen.

LEADER: Receive the blessing of the Spirit upon your feet. May you walk in the way of Christ all your days.

THOSE GATHERED: Amen.

The Peace

LEADER: The peace of God, the love of Christ, and the blessings of the Holy Spirit be with you all.

THOSE GATHERED: And also with you.

LEADER: Let us share the peace with one another.

SpiritGifts Covenant and Renewal Service

Opening Song

"Many Gifts, One Spirit"

Opening Words

Prayer

Scripture

Acts 1:1-8

Reflective Comments on Scripture

From what I have heard and shared, what does God want me to do or be in this week?
How does God invite me to change?

Certificate Presentation

As you are called by name, you will be presented with a certificate of completion.

LEADER: (Name), receive this certificate as a gifted child of God.

THOSE GATHERED: (Name), we recognize God's gifts in you and pray for the Holy Spirit's guidance upon you to live God's will all the days of your life.

The Blessing

87

The Peace

LEADER: The peace of God, the love of Christ, and the blessings of the Holy Spirit be with you all.

THOSE GATHERED: And also with you.

LEADER: Let us share the peace with one another.

88

Appendix

SpiritGifts Prayers

☞ The following prayers can be used at any time during the SpiritGifts program. You may wish to use one of them before each session. Other suggestions for use are provided in the SpiritGifts program guides found on pages 15-42. Feel free to adapt the prayers as you wish and to create your own prayers.

Empowering God, pour out your Spirit upon us, as you did on those gathered together on the day of Pentecost. Rush your wind upon us that we may be filled with your fire. Amen.

God of the Flame, burn in us. Today we count on your strength so that we can do your will. Ground us in the Holy Spirit so that we may live in truth and love. Amen.

God of Love, as you led the first disciples, now lead and strengthen us so that we may be your witnesses in (name your town or city) and (name your state) and to the ends of the earth. Amen.

God of History, we have seen the Holy Spirit work to bring your will on earth. Equip and empower us for the work of ministry. Amen.

Loving God, help us to make our hearts a dwelling place for your love. May your Spirit fill us with revealing light so that we may be a radiant beacon to the world. Amen.

Come, Holy Spirit, come. Enter our lives, free us from fear, and give us strength to carry on. Come, Holy Spirit, come. Give us the power to be your people. Amen.

Gracious One, give us hope and joy sufficient for the day. Impart your gifts that we may be the presence of Christ to the world. Help us to respond to the Spirit's leading and open ourselves to receive your gracious gifts. Amen.

Spirit of God, move within us so that we will be your witnesses to the world. Move among us, binding us together in love. Move through us, making us channels of God's love. Amen.

Praise be to God for the gifts to serve with one another. Praise be to the Spirit that binds us together in love. Amen.

Eternal Spirit, we thank you for the fire that burns within us, enflaming us to extend the love of Christ. Let us live now as Spirited people, ready to live God's will. Amen.

Source of All Unity, you are with us today and always. Show us how to live as builders of unity and makers of peace. In Christ's Spirit we pray. Amen.

Wonderful, amazing God, we have caught a glimpse of your will for us. That vision makes us restless, yearning for your fullest action in our lives. Make us your true daughters and sons through the power of your Holy Spirit. Amen.

God, since you are always present with us through your Spirit, we never despair. We rejoice at your continued healing in our lives. We thank you. We praise you. We worship you. Amen.

God of Wisdom, teach us to find the time and space for study and learning. Spirit of Truth, help us to balance our lives between action and reflection. Amen.

Music to Lift the Spirit: A Bibliography of Songs

☞ The following songs can be found in most new hymnals or collections of popular religious songs. Music is an integral part of the SpiritGifts program. Use these and other songs of your own choosing as often as you like throughout the program. Specific suggestions for using songs and music are provided in *How To Lead a SpiritGifts Program* (pages 10-14) and the *Spirit-Gifts Program Guides* (pages 15-42).

Three Key Songs

"Many Gifts, One Spirit." Words and music by Al Carmines, 1973.
This is the SpiritGifts theme song. Sing it at the beginning of the program and throughout as you find helpful. The song is included in both the *Participant's Workbook* (pages 12-13) and the *Leader's Resources* (pages 46-47).

"Spirit of the Living God." Words and music by Daniel Iverson, 1926.
This song can be substituted as the theme song or serve as a second theme song for your SpiritGifts program, if you wish. You may also want to create motions to use with the song.

"The Gift of Love." Words by Hal Hopson, 1972; music, traditional, adapted by Hal Hopson, 1972.
This song is a modern translation of 1 Corinthians 13, set to a traditional English melody that will be familiar to your ear. The song also can be led without accompaniment, with the leader singing each phrase and then inviting the participants to sing the phrase with her or him. Use this song after reading 1 Corinthians 13, the love chapter. You also may use the song in conjunction with the Responsive Listening Bible Study of the same text (pages 138-139).

Other Songs to Lift the Spirit

"All Praise to Our Redeeming Lord." Words by Charles Wesley; music by Sylvanus B. Pond, 1836.

"Christ, from Whom All Blessings Flow." Words by Charles Wesley; music adapted from Orlando Gibbons, 1623.

"Come, Holy Ghost, Our Hearts Inspire." Words by Charles Wesley, 1740; music from Est's *The Whole Book of Psalms*, 1592.

"Every Time I Feel the Spirit." African American spiritual.

"Filled with the Spirit's Power." Words by John R. Peacey, 1969; music by Cyril V. Taylor, 1943.

"God the Spirit, Guide and Guardian." Words by Carl P. Daw, Jr., 1987; music by Rowland H. Prichard, 1944.

"Help Us Accept Each Other." Words by Fred Kaan, 1974; music by John Ness Beck, 1977.

"Holy Spirit, Come, Confirm Us." Words by Brian Foley; music by V. Earle Copes, 1960.

"O Spirit of the Living God." Words by Henry H. Tweedy, 1935; music, traditional, arranged by Ralph Vaughn Williams, 1906.

"Sweet, Sweet Spirit." Words and music by Doris Akers, 1962.

"Wind Who Makes All Winds That Blow." Words by Thomas H. Troeger, 1983; music by Carol Doran, 1985.

SpiritGifts Bibliography of Resources

Discover Your Gifts: A Call to Discover and Use Your Spiritual Gifts. With Chuck Bradley. Church Growth 2000, 1978. Videocassette and discussion guide. This twenty-nine-minute video is the story of a reluctant church member who discovers and uses his gifts in Christ's service. Although the clothes date the video, the humor is timeless and the teachings are solid. Available from Church Growth, Inc., P.O. Box 541, Monrovia, CA 91017.

Edwards, Lloyd. *Discerning Your Spiritual Gifts.* Cambridge, Mass.: Cowley Publications, 1988. With sound theology and reasoning, this book is a good supplementary resource for use in workshops and retreats.

Harbaugh, Gary L. *God's Gifted People: Discovering Your Personality as a Gift.* Minneapolis: Augsburg Fortress, 1990. This text is an application of the Myers-Briggs Personality Type Indicator, the most widely used measure of personalities, dispositions, and preferences. It combines the gifts of the Spirit with psychological insights to search out reflections on faith and daily life.

Hawkins, Thomas R. *Claiming God's Promises: A Guide to Discovering Your Spiritual Gifts.* Nashville: Abingdon Press, 1992. This book includes a process for individuals as well as groups to progress toward a deeper spiritual life and broader ministry. The author explores biblical passages related to the gifts of ministry.

Kinghorn, Kenneth Cain. *Gifts of the Spirit.* Nashville: Abingdon Press, 1976. Kinghorn offers insights and advice about how to accept and use the gifts of God. The book goes beyond instruction to inspire, sharpen understanding, and stimulate commitment.

Page, Patricia N. *All God's People Are Ministers: Equipping Church Members for Ministry.* Minneapolis: Augsburg Fortress, 1993. The primary goal of this book is to strengthen laypeople in their ministry. It shows how the people of God can be helped to discover how important their ministry is and how they can be empowered to carry out their ministry.

Schmitt, Harley H. *Many Gifts, One Lord: A Biblical Understanding of the Variety of Spiritual Gifts Among the Early Christians and in the Church Today.* Minneapolis: Augsburg Fortress, 1993. An excellent scholarly resource that walks the reader through the New Testament passages pertaining to the gifts of the Spirit. The author then applies the gifts to contemporary life.

SpiritGifts News Release/Announcement

☞ This news release is provided as a model for you to adapt for use in publicizing your Spirit-Gifts program, whether it be a one-hour session, one-day workshop, weekend retreat, or multiple-week study. You also may wish to print a shortened version of the news release as an announcement in your newsletter and other congregational and community publications.

(Date)

What is God's will and purpose for my life? How can I serve God most effectively through the ministries of my congregation? Have you ever asked yourself one or both of these questions? If so, then SpiritGifts is for you. What is SpiritGifts? It is an exciting new program in which individuals join together in supportive community to discover their unique spiritual gifts and how they may use these gifts to further God's plan for their lives and their world.

(Write specific information here for your congregation or intended audience. Include the dates, times, and places for the SpiritGifts programs to be offered. Add a quotation of your own.)

(Signature of pastor or SpiritGifts leader)

A Letter to SpiritGifts Participants

☞ This is a suggested letter for you to send to those who express a desire to participate in SpiritGifts. You should send it only after you have made personal contact with the individual and have extended an invitation to participate in the program. The letter clarifies the purpose of the program and gives information regarding dates and times. Feel free to revise the letter as you wish to reflect your personal style.

(Date)

Dear _____,

It was a pleasure to talk with you about the opportunity to attend a SpiritGifts program. We are constantly searching for ways to help the people of *(name of your congregation)* find God's will and purpose for their lives. We also want to make sure that everyone can serve effectively through the ministries of our congregation.

What is SpiritGifts? SpiritGifts is a journey of spiritual growth in which individuals join together in supportive community to discover their unique spiritual gifts and how they may use these gifts to further God's plan for their lives and their world.

SpiritGifts will be offered *(list information regarding the dates, times, and places that SpiritGifts groups are scheduled to meet)*. A representative from the congregation will be calling soon to sign you up for the group that best fits your schedule and needs.

If you have any additional questions, please feel free to call me. We look forward to having you join us in this exciting program.

Sincerely,

(Your name)
(Your telephone number)

Notes

Notes

Notes

Notes

Notes